Along Alaskan Trails

Adventures in Sled Dog History

Helen Hegener
Northern Light Media

*Seward and Susitna mail team, 1913.
Photograph by Louis H. Pedersen.
National Postal Museum,
 Curatorial Photographic Collection*

Northern Light Media Books
Post Office Box 759
Palmer, Alaska 99645
http://northernlightmedia.com

© 2012 Northern Light Media

Front cover photograph of Bruce Linton, 2012 Iditarod, by Eric Vercammen.
Back cover photograph of Seavey's Iditaride Kennels sled dogs, by Eric Vercammen.

Copyright under International and Universal Copyright Conventions. All rights reserved. No part of this book may be reproduced or transmitted in any form or by any means, electronic or mechanical, including photocopying, recording, or by any information storage and retrieval system, without written permission from the copyright holder. Brief passages not to exceed 500 words may be quoted for reviews of this book.

Hegener, Helen
   Along Alaska Trails : Adventures in Sled Dog History / Helen Hegener
   ISBN 978-0-9843977-3-0   (ISBN-10 0-9843977-3-6)
   1. Alaska History. 2. Sled dogs.
   Includes appendixes: bibliography, resources, and index.

To order single copies of this book please send $20.00 (includes handling and shipping via Priority Mail) to the publisher: Northern Light Media, PO Box 759, Palmer, Alaska 99645-0759. Please make PayPal payments to helenhegener@gmail.com

Northern Light Media publishes books about sled dog history and races in Alaska. Other titles include *The All Alaska Sweepstakes, Yukon Quest Album, The Stained Glass Dogteam, 3,000 Miles to Nome (Sept, 2012)*, and the critically acclaimed DVD *Appetite and Attitude: A Conversation with Lance Mackey*.
http://northernlightmedia.com

Along Alaskan Trails

Adventures in Sled Dog History

Helen Hegener

"He who gives time to the study of the history of Alaska, learns that the dog, next to man, has been the most important factor in its past and present development."
                    -Judge James Wickersham (1938)

Leonhard Seppala with his favorite leader, Togo

Along Alaskan Trails

Introduction
    Heroic Dogs, Intrepid Men   8

Dogteam Delivery
    Sled Dog Mail   10

Jujiro Wada
    Enigma on the Trail   14

Seppala's Dogs
    Togo, Fritz and Balto   20

The Stained Glass Dog Team
    Historic Mushing Artwork   24

The Huskies and the Reindeer
    "treacherous, unreliable beasts"   28

Mary Joyce, Adventurer
Mushing from Juneau to Fairbanks   34

Olympic Sled Dogs
Mushing Luminaries Competed   38

All Alaska Sweepstakes
The Oldest Sled Dog Race   42

Ghosts of the Trail
Racing with Spirits   46

Split-the-Wind
"...the greatest musher..."   50

Military Sled Dogs
They Received the Croix de Guerre   54

Ernest de Koven Leffingwell
Mapping Alaska's Arctic Coastline   58

Alaska Highway Trailblazer
"...blue eyes that looked miles away..."   62

Archdeacon of the Yukon
10,000 Miles with a Dogsled   66

Baldy of Nome
Scotty Allan's Legendary Leader   70

A Dog-Puncher on the Yukon
Arthur Treadwell Walden   74

Appendixes
Bibliography, Resources   78

Index
Finding Everything   88

They were new dogs, utterly transformed by the harness. All passiveness and unconcern had dropped from them. They were alert and active, anxious that the work should go well, and fiercely irritable with whatever, by delay or confusion, retarded that work. The toil of the traces seemed the supreme expression of their being, and all that they lived for and the only thing in which they took delight.

~From *The Call of the Wild*, by Jack London

Prize Dog Team in the Arctic.

Introduction

The history of Alaska would be very different without the criss-crossing trails of thousands of sled dog teams. Man's dependence on these canine workhorses of the north can be seen in photo after photo: A dogteam carrying passengers on the Richardson Trail, a dogteam hauling freight across the Iditarod Trail, two dogteams loaded with the U.S. Mail and bound for Anchorage from Seward, a dogteam on patrol from Fort Gibbon near Tanana, a dogteam making its way along the frozen Yukon River to the next missionary stopover...

Sifting through hundreds of photos of Alaskan dogteams makes clear their important role in the history of this land. Before cars and trucks, there were sled dogs. Before ships, trains, and airplanes, there were sled dogs. In every part of this great land, from the misty fjords of southeastern Alaska to the farthest northern tip of the continent, sled dogs were the most dependable - and often the only - form of transportation.

In a slim collection of stories titled *Alaska Trail Dogs* (1945, Richard R. Smith), author Elsie Noble Caldwell cites a number which may or may not be accurate: "More than thirty-five thousand dogs have played a part in the development of Alaskan resources..."

Whatever their numbers, the importance of sled dogs in the history of the north is undisputed, and the stories in this book illustrate the many ways in which the dog team made travel and moving loads over otherwise impassable trails possible.

In *The Cruelest Miles* (2003, W.W. Norton & Co.) Gay and Laney Salisbury wrote: "On the Alaskan trail, sled dogs became partners in a game of survival. Drivers depended on their dogs so that they could make a living as freighters, mailmen, and trappers, and relied on the animals' skill and intelligence to get them safely across the rough, dangerous terrain."

Typical Alaskan sled dogs were not always the photogenic lot depicted in movies or on posters of Sgt. Preston of the Mounties with his faithful sidekick Yukon King. They were more often odd-sized, dock-tailed, and funny-colored, for as the Salisburys noted, "The demand for sled dogs was so high, particularly during the northern gold rushes, that the supply of dogs ran out and a black market for dogs sprang up in the states. Any dog that looked as if it could pull a sled or carry a saddlebag--whether or not it was suited to withstand the cold--was kidnapped and sold in the north."

In his book, *Ten Thousand Miles with a Dog Sled* (1914, Charles Scribner's), gold-rush era missionary Hudson Stuck wrote that the original Native sled dogs had been extensively mated with setters, pointers, hounds, mastiffs, Saint Bernards and Newfoundlands, creating "a general admixture of breeds, so that the work dogs of Alaska are a heterogeneous lot..."

Despite their often questionable backgrounds, most sled dogs share a love of being on the trail and going someplace new with their teammates and their driver, a term which originated with drivers of oxen and horses, but by which mushers have always been known in Alaska. Sled dogs were, and still are, working animals, but according to their nature and in keeping with their role as Man's Best Friend, sled dogs were often much more than just beasts of burden. When Scotty Allen was elected to the Alaska Legislature and moved to the capitol city of Juneau, his faithful lead dog Baldy, who had once saved his life, went along. And when Scotty Allan retired to California, once again Baldy accompanied his master along strange and unknown trails. Leonhard Seppala was rarely without the faithful Togo, until he retired his peerless leader to a life of comfort with his friend Elizabeth Ricker.

In an often unforgiving land of intrepid men and heroic dogs it was not uncommon to find a trail-wise husky at the heels of almost any miner, trapper, logger, hunter, surveyor, explorer, or any other reason a man found to be in the wilds of Alaska. Many men's lives depended on the speed and intelligence of these dogs, and many courageous men cried when they lost one of their faithful team members. From the wise leaders who could find a trail buried in a blizzard, to the strong wheel dogs who could shift an entire sled out of danger in an instant, each dog in every team was an important part of the writing of Alaska's history.

Today's sled dog races are a continuing testament to the courage and stamina of these incredibly tough animals, showcasing their continuing endurance and exhibiting their sheer joyous love of running. The sled dogs running today's races are very often the direct descendants of canine royalty, strong brave dogs who worked side-by-side with the men who built Alaska. A few of their stories are in this book.   ~•~

U.S. Mail being delivered by dogteam. Photo by Harry T. Becker.
Harry T. Becker Photograph Collection P67-0376 Alaska State Library

Dogteam Delivery

Sled Dog Mail

Delivering the mail in Alaska has always presented a formidable challenge to the U.S. Postal Service. Letters, parcels, and supplies from the "lower 48 states" often took weeks or months to reach their destinations. Steamships transported Alaska bound mail north from Puget Sound in Washington to southeastern coastal towns. After reaching these towns, mail was carried to some sections of interior Alaska by river steamers and, later, by Alaska Railroad trains for delivery to smaller, outlying villages.

The harsh Arctic weather and limited trail and road system also made mail delivery extremely difficult. In the more isolated sections, carrying the mail required methods far different than those traditionally used elsewhere in the United States. Dogs proved superior for the winter transport of mail. Dogs were capable of covering long distances, day or night, and could travel over frozen lakes and rivers and pass through dense forests.

The native Alaskan malamute or husky was the most valued dog for teams, as having been born and bred in the north, they were strong, with thick coats and furry paws, and thrived on dried salmon and needed no special housing. Because of the high demand for sled dogs during the gold rush era, other breeds such as Newfoundlands, St. Bernards, setters, spaniels, and collies were also used. As in earlier frontiers, horses were also used in Alaska, but they posed special problems, as feed was costly and hard to supply and horses required special care in the extreme cold temperatures of winter.

By 1901, a network of mail trails throughout Alaska was in use, including a system following almost the entire length of the Yukon River. The historic Iditarod Trail was the main dog trail that carried mail from Seward to Nome, with over-night roadhouses along the route which served mail carriers, freighters, and other travelers who used sled dog teams.

Mail dogteams varied in size, with eight to twelve dogs the most common number for pulling a mail sled, which was often heavier and longer than a typical basket-style sled. On average, dog teams pulled sleds containing between 500 – 700 pounds of mail, which meant that each dog had a load of up to 100 pounds (although they hauled less on the more challenging trails). Mail sacks usually weighed 50 pounds each. Rubber-lined waterproof bags were used to

U.S. Mail dogteam on the Yukon River. Photographer P.S. Hunt.
John Zug Album UAF 1980-68-252 University of Alaska Fairbanks

Seward and Susitna mail team, 1913. Photograph by Louis H. Pedersen.
National Postal Museum, Curatorial Photographic Collection

protect precious mail from snow, rain, and mud; the dogs often wore moosehide moccasins to protect their feet as much as possible from jagged pieces of ice.

In the 1930s airplanes became the most popular means for mail transport, but dogteams were still used to make "feeder" deliveries to remote locations in bush Alaska. Postmasters were also still allowed to use dogs for "emergency mail service" to rural points, and the Postmaster General had the authority to build and maintain trails and facilities and to hire contracted mail teams without going through a lengthy bid process. In the 1940s cachets were produced reading "Alaska Dog Team Post" and depicting adventurous-looking artwork of dogteams in action. These beautifully illustrated cachets, which were fairly common during the WWII years, are prized today by collectors of sled dog memorabilia.

In 1963, the U.S. Post Office Department honored Chester Noongwook of Savoonga, on St. Lawrence Island in the Bering Sea, as the last driver to officially deliver the U.S. Mail via dogteam. With his retirement, regular sled dog mail delivery ended in Alaska. A photo by early Alaskan photographer Ward Wells depicts fur trader Ed Shepherd and Nathan Noongwook shaking hands above a flag which reads "The Adventurers Club," in front of a sled in the village of Gambell, on St. Lawrence Island. The sled is being prepared for last U.S. mail run by dogsled in Alaska, to be driven by Chester Noongwook, son of Nathan Noongwook, from Gambell to Savoonga, also on St. Lawrence Island. In January 1995, Chester Noongwook donated the mail-delivery sled he used on that historic final run to the National Postal Museum in Washington, DC. The last official U.S. Mail sled dog driver, Chester Noongwook passed away only one month after making the delivery.

Along Alaskan Trails

In 1986 the U.S. Postal System issued a seventeen-cent stamp as part of its transportation series, in recognition of the important role the dogsled played in early mail delivery in the north. A simple image of a basket sled, the type often used for transporting mail across Alaskan trails, is under the words "Dog Sled 1920s." Iditarod champion Susan Butcher took part in the first-day issue ceremony in Anchorage when the stamp was released.

On January 2, 2009 the U.S. Postal Service issued a new First Class stamp commemorating Alaska's 50th anniversary as a U.S. State (Alaska became an official U.S. territory in 1912 and the 49th state on January 3, 1959). The image selected, which was photographed by official Iditarod Trail Sled Dog Race photographer Jeff Schultz, depicts veteran sled dog racer Dee Dee Jonrowe on the Iditarod Trail at sunset, near Rainy Pass in the Alaska Range, during the 2000 Iditarod Trail Sled Dog Race. It was a fitting scene for an Alaskan commemorative stamp, evoking images of the dogteams which covered the Iditarod Trail and many others to bring letters, cards, and news of loved ones to those in far away places. ~•~

Postcard printed for the Alaska-Yukon-Pacific Exposition held in Seattle in 1909:
"Ben Atwater, arriving at Lake Bennett from Circle City with U.S. Mail, Alaska."

Jujiro Wada

Enigma on the Trail

There are many strange and unusual stories in the annals of northern sled dog travel, but one of the most fascinating concerns an enigmatic Japanese explorer and adventurer named Jujiro Wada. Born in Japan in the 1870s, the second son of a lower-class samurai warrior, he traveled to the U.S. in 1890 and worked as a cabin boy for the Pacific Steam Whaling Company and at Barrow for the renowned Charlie Brower, manager of the Cape Smythe Whaling and Trading Company, which was probably where he learned how to handle a sled dog team and to speak Alaska Native languages.

Jujiro Wada was with E.T. Barnette when the businessman landed at what is now the site of Fairbanks. Hearing about the recent gold strikes nearby, Barnette dispatched Wada up the

Yukon River with one of Barnette's own dogteams, taking the first news of the strikes to the miners at Dawson City. Wada drove Barnette's team into Dawson City on Dec. 28, 1902, and upon interviewing him the *Yukon Sun* printed a front-page story with the bold headline, "Rich Strike Made in the Tanana."

Several hundred miners quickly left Dawson City for Fairbanks, but most were disappointed to find the best sites were already staked. As the story goes, an angry mob gathered at Barnette's store and threatened violence against both Barnette and Wada. An article in the *Dawson Daily News*, July 8, 1912, mentioned Wada's legendary predicament:

"Jujiro Wada, the mushing Jap who brought the first news of the Fairbanks strike to Dawson, and has made numerous other trips in the North, recently blew into Fairbanks again with a new story about the placer country of Western Alaska. The *Times* says: Ten years in a placer camp is a long, long time, more than five or ten times that number of years in an older community, where things move more slowly and the population does not come and go with such kaleidoscopic changes. Thus, the return of Jujiro Wada to Fairbanks might be likened almost to the return of one of the Pilgrim fathers to Plymouth, in point of the changes that have taken place in Fairbanks and the generations (placer camp generations) that have come and gone since he first visited the section and then mushed overland to Dawson ten years ago, with the news that caused the Fairbanks stampede. True, when the Dawsonites moved over the winter trail and viewed Felix Pedro's strike the majority of them were in favor of hanging Wada, but the hardy little brown musher has since been vindicated. His estimate of the camp was the correct one, and those of that first stampede who remained have mostly prospered. Thus it always gives him much satisfaction to drop back to Fairbanks and view the progress."

Five years earlier, however, in a *Dawson Daily News* article dated September 1907, Wada had already explained what actually happened:

"The story that I was about to be hanged for causing a thought-to-be-fake stampede was not correct. The fact is that the miners held a meeting to decide as to the price of flour then being offered by one of the trading companies. They thought the price exorbitant. It was rumored that the miners had a rope on my neck, and were about to hoist me. Now that is not true. The other part of the story, that I showed a copy of the (Seattle) *Post-Intelligencer* saying

"The return of Mr. Wada after a 1,680-mile mush over snow and ice."
Adams Photo, Dawson City, Yukon Territory, 1908

that several years before I had rescued a party of shipwrecked whalers in the Arctic in dead of winter is true. I did show that paper to let some of the boys know I had been up North, but it was not in a plea to save my neck."

For many years Jujiro Wada traveled widely across northern Alaska, the Yukon Territory, and beyond, leading an adventurous life and leaving his mark on the history of the north country. His exploits were the stuff of legend, as he traveled by dog team, hunting, trapping, prospecting, running marathons, and entertaining people wherever he went with his colorful stories. On one of his epic dog mushing trips he travelled from the headwaters of the Chandalar River to the Arctic Ocean, along the shore of the ocean to the Mackenzie River, and up that river and across the divide to the Porcupine River, taking more than a year, he and his dogs living on game hunted along the way.

Another of Wada's lasting contributions to Alaskan history was helping to pioneer the Iditarod Trail after several gold strikes were made in the Iditarod area, although in most accounts of Wada's travels the trip appears as something of a footnote to his other adventures. In a summary of Yuji Tani's 1995 book, *The Samurai Dog-Musher Under the Northern Lights*, Fumi Torigai, who was documenting Wada's travels for submission to the Historic Sites and Monuments Board of Parks Canada, wrote:

Jujiro Wada with his friend, Captain H.H. Norwood of the whaling ship Balaena, 1903.

"In December of 1909, at the request of the town, Wada established a route from Seward to the newly discovered gold mine of Iditarod. Acting as the leader of a fleet of dogsled teams, Wada had a relatively uneventful trip to Iditarod. However, on the return trip to Seward, he and his three companions had to go through prolonged minus 60 F (minus 51 C) weather. Several dogs, including his lead-dog, became too weak to survive the extreme cold and had to be put to sleep. The hardships of Wada and his companions and the ensuing rush of prospectors into the Iditarod area were widely reported in many Alaskan papers."

In early 1912, Wada was in the Kuskokwim area, looking for traces of a Japanese man known locally as Allen, who had disappeared there. On March 11, 1912, Wada was in Iditarod. In July 1912, he and his partner, John Baird, made a gold strike on the Tulasak River. Wada took about $12,000 in gold with him when he went to Seattle to report the findings to his backers, who included Edward Avery McIlhenny of Tabasco sauce fame and the Guggenheim brothers.

Along Alaskan Trails

Excerpts from an article which appeared in the *Dawson Daily News*, July 8, 1912:

Wada Tells of the Country to the West

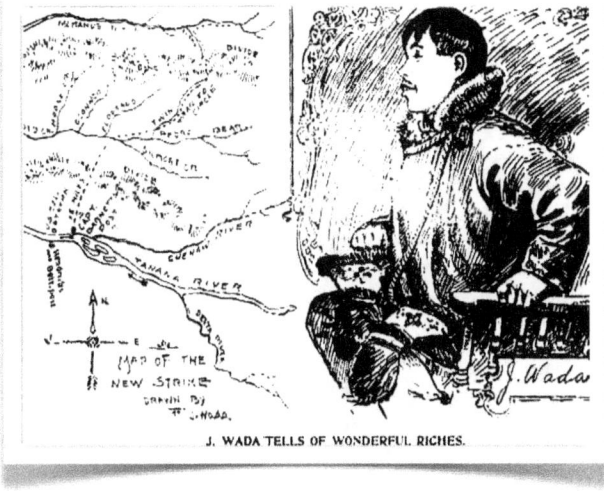

J. WADA TELLS OF WONDERFUL RICHES.

Jujiro Wada, the mushing Jap who brought the first news of the Fairbanks strike to Dawson, and has made numerous other trips in the North, recently blew into Fairbanks again with a new story about the placer country of Western Alaska, the Times says:

Wada was in Fairbanks a few years ago during the revival of Marathon racing, and figured in several of the big contests, but he left shortly after the great Fourth of July Marathon of 1909 when, before the largest crowd ever gathered at Fairbanks, Jerry Sullivan, of Nome, with his musher's trot, came home with the money. Since that date until Saturday night Wada has found time to cover considerable stretches of Northland, besides spending almost a year in the States.

One of Wada's Alaskan stunts since leaving Fairbanks was the blazing of the overland trail to the Iditarod from Seward. He was hired to do this by the town of Seward and returning, reported that the route was feasible and that the Iditarod would make a good small camp. The road commission has since followed Wada's route. The next year found Wada down in the States, where almost the first person he met was a now wealthy ex-senator from Texas, whom Wada had known twenty years before up near Point Barrow, just after the Texan had graduated from college. The two held the big talkfest and then they took in the East together, not forgetting the Great White Way at New York. After almost a year in the States under the direction of his old Point Barrow friend, Wada hied himself North once more, backed by the man from Texas whom he now represents and whom he is to meet at New Orleans when he gets outside on his present trip.

The first point visited last year after leaving San Francisco was Good News Bay, near the mouth of the Kuskokwim. Wada remained there until last November, when he heard of the Aniak river strike, when he moved up river and investigated that country. Still later he stampeded back down river to the Tulasak river and got in on the ground along Bear creek.

Returning to the Iditarod from the Tulasak, Wada took Jack Baird, formerly of Fairbanks, with him and, moving a prospecting drill, the two crossed over to the Kuskokwim in the spring and proceeded to test some of the ground on Bear creek. The indications were very favourable, hence Wada's trip out to New Orleans to lay his findings before his backer.

To judge by the bottle of coarse gold that Wada carries with him, taken from Bear creek, some of the nuggets being worth $10, it is evident that the prospectors secured more than indications.

From the tests made by Baird and Wada the little brown musher is well satisfied that Bear creek will soon be famous as a dredging camp, for there is plenty of gold on bedrock. In fact, the Kuskokwim Commercial company will be one of the outfits that will put a dredge on Bear creek this summer. Wada does not know who their backers are.

Referring to the Aniak river, which empties into the Kuskokwim about 75 miles above Tulasak, and which heads back against the same mountain as Bear creek, Wada predicts the men on Marble creek will have a good little camp.

Jujiro Wada

The Seward Museum has a three-part video series online telling the story of the Iditarod Trail expedition of Jujiro Wada, in newspaper articles read by Lee Poleske, president of the Resurrection Bay Historical Society. Recorded as part of the Iditarod Trail Centennial celebration, the free video series, available online, is informative and brings to light some of the history of this little-known Alaskan wanderer.

An article in the Sept. 13, 2009 *Fairbanks News-Miner*, by Ronald Inouye, titled "Jujiro Wada: musher, long distance runner and Fairbanks co-founder?," poses a critical inquiry:

"Why don't we know more about this remarkable individual? His feats and tenacity are exemplary although detractors question some of his motives and willingness to be manipulated by people like E.T. Barnette. Wada wished to become a U.S. citizen so he could own land and stake claims, but his application was denied. Later, during World War I he was accused of being a Japanese spy, but those charges were not confirmed.

"The newspaper accounts of those times, as now, are selective, likely reflecting the socio-economic conditions and attitudes of that era. Whereas Northerners then as now accept most individuals based on individual abilities, it has not always been so by federal standards. Alaska Natives were only accorded U.S. citizenship in 1915, and then only provisionally. Until 1922, non-whites weren't allowed citizenship through naturalization. These factors might have obscured the presence and exploits of individuals like Wada."

The 2007 Yukon Quest honored Wada with an exhibit of photos and newspaper clippings of his achievements in the north. The official press release read in part: "'Mr. Wada traveled by dog team along what is now the Yukon Quest Trail over 100 years ago when it was a traditional travel route. He learned his survival skills and travel routes through the assistance of the aboriginal people in the north,' said Lillian Nakamura Maguire, educator for the Yukon Human Rights Commission. "'He was respected for his hardiness, dog care and good character, although, as a Japanese man he experienced racism due to the strong anti-Asian sentiments in the early 1900s,' Nakamura Maguire said.

"'The Yukon Quest is dedicated to honouring the traditions of travel by dog team in the North and the equal treatment of all dogs and people taking part in the race. Mr. Wada embodied the love and respect for his dogs that is one of the founding principles of the Yukon Quest,' said Stephen Reynolds, Yukon Quest (Canada) Executive Director. 'We are honoured to help bring Jujiro Wada's incredible story to the world.'"

In an article for the *Fairbanks News-Miner* in June, 2011, author and historian Dermot Cole wrote: "Jujiro Wada, who promoted many mining ventures, traveled great distances across Alaska by dog team. He also helped blaze the trail from Seward to Iditarod."

In 1912, the *News-Miner* took note of the rocky reception given to Wada in early 1903 and explained what transpired afterwards in an article which helped to secure his status as an explorer, adventurer, and intrepid musher: "True, when the Dawsonites moved over the winter trail and viewed Felix Pedro's strike the majority of them were in favor of hanging Wada, but the hardy little brown musher has since been vindicated. His estimate of the camp was the correct one and those of that first stampede who remained have mostly prospered."

The online encyclopedia Wikipedia details Wada's continuing travels in later life:

"Wada returned to Seward in November 1912. He brought with him two sled loads of mining equipment, another sled load of miscellaneous supplies, and four Japanese companions who would serve as assistant dog drivers. The Japanese and their twenty dogs then drove to the Bear Creek strike. Wada remained at the Bear Creek site until February 1913.

"Wada went to Seattle for a short while, then he returned to Alaska in May 1913. That same year, he was described in John Underwood's Alaska, an Empire in the Making as one of Alaska's best long-distance dog sled drivers.

"In 1915, a man named Ernest Blue wrote in the Cordova Daily Times that Wada was a Japanese spy, asserting that Blue had seen cash and a map of Alaska in Wada's possession. This story reappeared in 1923 and during WWII. During May 1915, Wada was in San Pedro, California, working at Van Camp's tuna packing plant, but left town swiftly after receiving a phone call. As with many stories about Wada, the published accounts are contradictory. In the Seattle Times on May 15, 1916, Wada insisted the phone call was a job offer in Alaska, and he traveled to New York. However, on page 217 of Tani, 1995, Wada wrote a letter to his friend Sunada, written on Van Camp Sea Food Company stationery. that reads, "Sorry to say but I am compelled to leave here... otherwise they will kill me."

"During 1917-1918, Wada resumed prospecting in the Yukon, mostly along High Cache Creek. In 1919, he went to the Northwest Territories.

"On September 6, 1920, he entered New York State via Niagara Falls. He listed his last residence as Herschel Island, Northwest Territories, and his employer as E.F. Lufkin. He listed his height as 5'2", his hair as black, and his complexion as dark.

"From 1920-1923, he was trapping foxes on the Upper Porcupine. He also searched for gold around Herschel Island and for oil around Fort Norman (modern Norman Wells). His business partners during this time included the veteran trader Poole Field.

"Wada left Canada in April 1923. On May 3, 1923, he arrived at Ketchikan aboard the SS Princess Mary. He listed himself as a citizen of Canada, but was not allowed entry into Alaska because he had no passport.

"His subsequent whereabouts are not currently documented, but in 1930, he was in Chicago, Illinois. In May 1934, he was in Seattle, having recently arrived from San Francisco. During January 1936, he was in Green River, Wyoming. During the winter of 1936-1937, he was in Redding, California.

"He died at the San Diego County hospital on March 5, 1937. The cause of death was listed as peritonitis caused by diverticulitis."

Jujiro Wada was buried in an unmarked grave. A large bronze monument to the far-wandering traveler was established in 2007 in a park in Matsuyama City, Japan, celebrating the high points of his adventurous life.   ~•~

Togo, 1925 Serum Run leader

Seppala's Dogs

Togo, Fritz and Balto

Legendary Alaskan dog driver Leonhard Seppala cuts a giant swath across sled dog racing history, often photographed in his signature squirrel-skin parka, with his handsome huskies beside him. Born in Norway, Seppala emigrated to Alaska during the gold rush and learned to drive dogs by hauling freight and supplies for the mines around Nome. His kennel partner in later years, Elizabeth M. Ricker, described Sepp as "a modest, unassuming character," but she also unhesitatingly defines him as "King of the Alaskan Trail."

Seppala entered his first All Alaska Sweepstakes race in 1914, but being unfamiliar with the trail, he made a grave miscalculation and lost. He returned the following year and won, and he won again in 1916 and 1917, equaling the record of another great dog driver, A.A. "Scotty" Allan. When the 1925 diphtheria epidemic threatened Nome -- and Sepp's own daughter -- he and his dauntless team travelled over 260 miles in "The Great Race of Mercy," and thereby secured their place in history.

Along Alaskan Trails

The most famous dog in Seppala's kennel, Balto, was not supposed to be in the Serum Run; in fact, he'd never even led a team before. He was a freighting dog, slower than the racing dogs needed for speedy delivery of the serum, and Seppala had selected against including him in the team when he left Nome. It was only when the Governor of Alaska, in an unexpected move, decided to speed up the relay by authorizing the addition of more teams and drivers to Seppala's leg at the end, that Sepp's young assistant, a Norwegian named Gunnar Kaasen, chose the big black Balto, whom he had long favored and whose merit he wanted to prove, to lead his team in the final leg of the relay.

Seppala's easy choice had been his older, trusted leader, a small, tough husky called Togo. He was a Siberian husky with a black, brown, cream and gray coat, and he weighed less than 50 pounds. But what Togo lacked in size he made up for in heart, and Seppala considered Togo his best sled dog, a strong and determined leader. Sepp wrote "I can safely say that he has won more races than any dog in Alaska." Named after a Japanese Admiral, Seppala often said that Togo was "the best dog that ever traveled the Alaskan trail" and "I never had a better dog than Togo."

The largely unsung hero of Seppala's kennel, Togo's half-brother and also a veteran of the Serum Run, was Fritz. Born in 1915 and bred by Seppala, Fritz was a cream-colored Siberian husky with a mottled brown and gray saddle, neck and head markings, who became an important foundation sire in early Siberian husky pedigrees. He often led Seppala's team in

Leonhard Seppala with his 1925 Serum Run
co-leaders, half brothers Togo and Fritz.

A weary Balto stands at the head of Gunnar Kassen's team on Front Street in Nome, shortly after finishing the final leg of the serum run on February 2, 1925.

tandem with Togo in races and on cross-country jaunts, and during the Serum Run he was co-leading with Togo. In Elizabeth Ricker's biographical book, *Seppala, Alaskan Dog Driver*, Leonhard Seppala called Fritz "a great dog." He proved his greatness by becoming an important foundation sire of the early Siberian husky breed, which was officially recognized by the American Kennel Club in 1930.

In an interesting series of coincidences, Balto, Togo and Fritz were all mounted after they died, and they each travelled long and winding paths to their final resting places. The only one of the three who returned to their birthplace, Fritz was purchased and returned to Nome and is prominently featured in the Carrie McLain museum. Togo is on display at the Iditarod Trail Sled Dog Race headquarters cabin in Wasilla, Alaska, while Balto is at the Cleveland Museum of Natural History in Cleveland, Ohio.

At the end of Elizabeth Ricker's book, Leonhard Seppala writes about leaving his old friend Togo in her care, and it must have been difficult for him to write the final lines: "It seemed best to leave him ... where he could enjoy a well-earned rest. But it was a sad parting on a cold gray March morning when Togo raised a small paw to my knee as if questioning why he was not going along with me. For the first time in twelve years I hit the trail without Togo."

Balto, the dog who wasn't even supposed to be in a Serum Run team, went on to become one of the most widely recognized and beloved sled dogs in history. Books, movies, photos, games, toys and much more celebrate the heroic efforts of the dogteams who saved Nome, and for better or worse, Balto became the iconic lead dog whose name would evoke bravery, loyalty and dedication. Generations of schoolkids learned the story of the intrepid sled dog who struggled through a blizzard to deliver the anti-toxin, and while some specific details may not be historically accurate, the legacy is not totally misplaced.

On the bronze statue which was erected to honor Balto in New York City's Central Park, a plaque is inscribed with a tribute to all of the Serum Run sled dogs:

> *Dedicated to the indomitable spirit of the sled dogs that*
> *relayed antitoxin six hundred miles over rough ice, across*
> *treacherous waters, through Arctic blizzards from Nenana*
> *to the relief of stricken Nome in the winter of 1925.*
> *Endurance · Fidelity · Intelligence*

Leonhard Seppala with Fritz

Stained Glass Dog Team

Historic Mushing Artwork

Sorting through Internet files while doing research for another book produced a link to an unusual piece of artwork, a dog team in stained glass which once graced a building in downtown Seattle, Washington. The image is compelling, utilizing an advanced stained glass technique which includes painting the faces of the driver, his passenger, and the huskies which make up the dog team. A Seattle photographer, Joe Mabel, took the photo which appears on a page at the Internet's Wikipedia, and when contacted he offered a little history of the glasswork:

"It dates from about 1910, and until some time in the 1980's it was part of the Alaskan Cigar Store in the building that was originally the old Arctic Club and is now low-income housing and a shelter, under the name Morrison Hotel (across Third Avenue from the King County Courthouse). Two companion stained glass pieces are still there, but they are less interesting. Seattle's Museum of History and Industry (MOHAI) probably knows a bit more, and definitely has a 'wall text' placard that shows a photo of the stained glass piece in its original location; the store itself had a bit of a setback from the street (with a sidewalk-facing display window), and the dog-sled piece now at MOHAI was about 8 feet away from the sidewalk, over the actual door."

The history of the building is an obscure but interesting bit of Alaskana, detailed at the HistoryLink, a free online encyclopedia of Washington history. An article by Jennifer Ott (2008) explains how The Alaska Club was organized in 1903 with the object of promoting Alaska and its resources, an idea which subsequently grew to include the Yukon and the Pacific. The group was largely responsible for the famous Alaska-Yukon-Pacific Exposition, which opened in Seattle on June 1, 1909. The HistoryLink article explains what happened next: "In April 1908, the

Alaska Club merged with the Arctic Club, a social club for Alaskans in Seattle. The new organization kept the name of the Arctic Club and combined the social nature of that club with the promotional efforts of the Alaska Club."

The Arctic Club opened in 1909, at the corner of 3rd Avenue and Jefferson Street. The Arctic Construction Company, a separate corporation with many investors from the Arctic Club, built the building. The new Arctic Club building was an astonishing piece of architecture, even for the grandiose times, and the September 14, 1912 issue of the *Pacific Builder and Engineer* described the building as the "richest and most commodious home of any social organization west of Chicago."

In 1914 a conflict between the club and the construction company led the club to relocate to the Arctic Building at 3rd Avenue and Cherry Street. Unable to leave their old bar behind, several of the members stole the bar from the old building by hoisting it out the window, and then installed it at the new building without telling anyone how they had obtained it. They later paid the Arctic Construction for it.

The National Register of Historic Places for Seattle website has an interesting description of the Arctic Club which was originally housed in the building: "The Arctic Building is associated with one of the lesser-known facets of the Klondike gold rush–the formation of social institutions for the men who returned from the Yukon gold rush after 'striking it rich.' Though most who headed north found no gold, a small percentage did return to Seattle with more than just memories. The Arctic Club, originally located in the Morrison Hotel, provided an exclusive social community for those Seattleites who had returned from the Alaska Gold Rush with money in their pockets and a repertoire of stories to tell about their adventures in the Yukon. In 1916, they commissioned A. Warren

Left: The artwork at the Arctic Club at Third and Jefferson, Seattle.

Gould, one of the city's most prominent architects, to design the building that would become their institution's new home."

The building's history was further described in this *Forensic Geneology* piece: "The Morrison began life as the New Arctic Hotel Building, whose doors opened in October of 1909. The largest social club in Seattle, the Arctic Club occupied half of the building. It is claimed, with apparent justness, the Arctic Club has the richest and most commodious home of any social organization west of Chicago, reported a magazine in 1912. By 1916 the Arctic Club outgrew its home at Third and Jefferson. They moved to the newly constructed Arctic Building on Third and Cherry. The New Arctic Hotel building then became the Hotel Seward, advertising rooms to let by the night or week. In 1934 it changed ownership and became the Hotel Morrison, which offered 300 up-to-date rooms from $1 and up."

The stained glass dog team was not mentioned in the architectural descriptions, but there were brief descriptions of the secondary stained glass pieces, such as in the Seattle Department of Neighborhoods Historical Sites Summary for 501 3rd Avenue: "Other notable exterior features include the stained glass window in the transom of the southern storefront on Third Avenue, featuring a mountain range above forest and the word 'Alaskan…'"

When an article about the stained glass dog team appeared in the online newsmagazine *Alaska Dispatch*, a reader, Justin Ivey, commented on what happened when the artwork was removed from the Morrison Hotel building: "My studio did the restoration of these windows for MOHAI prior to them being installed there. They were completely disassembled and rebuilt with new lead. We were required to heavily document the process, due to their historic nature. They were in pretty bad shape, with a fair amount of missing and broken glass."

A 2011 visit to the Seattle Museum of History and Industry (MOHAI) showed the window prominently displayed, with a placard which read: "Stained Glass Windows, ca. 1910. Conservation of stained glass supported in part by Seattle Stained Glass. These stained glass window panels graced the front of the Alaskan Cigar Store and Cafe in the original Arctic Club building near Pioneer Square. It is also believed the windows once hung in the Snoqualmie Bar, a local saloon that operated at the corner of First Avenue and Pike Street."

Justin Ivey, the designer/project manager at Seattle Stained Glass Inc., shared these photos of the restoration project with the author a few years ago, commenting: "We were hired by MOHAI several years ago to restore the windows. The documentation process consisted of making full scale rubbings of the original design, which we turned into patterns for the re-build. The windows were disassembled, cleaned and rebuilt with new lead that matched the profile of the original. Broken glass was cobbled together or replaced with appropriate matches where necessary, and the patterns were labeled any place that glass was replaced. All of the documentation and patterns were placed in the crates with the windows and delivered to the museum." ~•~

Justin Ivey, designer and project manager at Seattle Stained Glass, shared these photos of the restoration of the stained glass dog team. The artwork now hangs in Seattle's Museum of History and Industry with a placard showing its original location at the Arctic Club.

Alaska Reindeer, Kotzebue Herd No. 2. Lomen Bros. photo.
George A. Parks P240-215 Alaska State Library

The Huskies and the Reindeer

"...treacherous and unreliable beasts..."

    The colorful history of sled dog travel has been well documented over the years, in books ranging from the classic *Gold, Men and Dogs,* by A.A. Scotty Allen (G.P. Putnam Sons, 1931); to Archdeacon of the Yukon Hudson Stuck's *Ten Thousand Miles with a Dogsled* (1914). But one of the most compelling books ever written about sled dog travel in the north country is a newer title, published in 2003 by W.W. Norton & Company. *The Cruelest Miles: The Heroic Story of Dogs and Men in a Race Against an Epidemic,* by cousins Gay Salisbury and Laney Salisbury, details the heroic relay dash of twenty men and more than two hundred dogs who raced across 674 miles of Alaskan backcountry to deliver lifesaving serum and save the citizens of Nome fom a diphtheria outbreak. The book includes some wonderful history of the state, and at one point the Salisbury cousins note the central role of sled dogs in the history and development of the territory of Alaska: "...It was dogs and dog traction, for centuries the mainstay of Eskimo survival, that made this new world run. During the gold rushes, dogs brought the modern world to Alaska, hauling food, mining supplies, medicine, passengers, and gold across the network of rivers and trails that Eskimos and Athabaskans had been following for hundreds of years."

Then, in the next paragraph, the Salisburys report a little-known aspect of Alaskan history: "In addition to trade goods, the gold rush brought some strange ideas to Alaska, and the most bizarre may have been the belief of some U.S. government officials that Alaskans would be better off living in Alaska without dogs. Ambitious entrepreneurs tried many alternative forms of transportation and communication that they hoped would be superior to dogs, including horses, goats, hot-air balloons, bicycles, ice skates, ice boats, ice trains. and passenge pigeons. But the favorite choice of several key officials was the reindeer."

Incredibly, the primary proponent for reindeer was Dr. Sheldon Jackson, a Presbyterian minister and the head of Alaska's fledgling education system at the turn of the century. A staunch supporter of reindeer who argued their qualities far and wide, Jackson even testified before Congress that dogs were "treacherous and unreliable beasts," and claimed that they

An old photo of reindeer teams leaving Anvik Mission with 1,023 pounds of mail bound for Kaltag, December 27, 1920. Photo: Rev. J.W. Chapman
Rev. J.W. Chapman Collection P86-004 Alaska State Library

Dr. Sheldon H. Jackson, General Agent of Education, Territory of Alaska

Rev. Hudson Stuck Archdeacon of the Yukon

"require considerable food for their support, while reindeer are gentle, timid and eat little, foraging on the moss and spruce of the tundra."

Fortunately for our canine friends, the aforementioned Archdeacon Hudson Stuck challenged Jackson's assertions. He'd written compellingly in *Ten Thousand Miles With a Dogsled* that the husky dog was prized and called "the Friend of Man," and he observed "There is not a dog the less in Alaska because of the reindeer, nor ever will be..."

When the Canadian government introduced reindeer into Labrador under the direction of Dr. Wilfred Grenfell, who stated his hope they would "eliminate that scourge of the country, the husky dog," the Archdeacon Stuck responded, "Instead of the reindeer eliminating the dog, there is far greater likelihood of the dog eliminating the reindeer..."

After a few side paragraphs on feeding and caring for reindeer as opposed to dogs, the Archdeacon went on, warming to the argument: "Speaking broadly, the reindeer is a stupid, unwieldy, and intractable brute, not comparing for a moment with the dog in intelligence or adaptability." He did, however, admit to the reindeer's usefulness in one regard: "Wherein lies the success of the reindeer experiment in Alaska? Chiefly in the provision of a regular meat supply..."

But back to the history and how the situation reached such an impasse. During the later half of the 1800's, whaling ships traveled extensively along the Bering Sea coast of Alaska as traders found a native populace willing to exchange their pelts, hides and meat of the resident marine mammals for guns, ammunition, tobacco, alcohol, and foods like sugar and flour. So great was the impact of these negotiations, when coupled with wildlife populations diminished by poaching and various other reasons, that by 1888 Captains of the U. S. Revenue Cutter Service ships which patrolled the waters of western Alaska became concerned for the well being of the Native Alaskans living along the Bering Sea villages.

Dr. Sheldon Jackson, a Presbyterian minister and the Commissioner of Education in Alaska, joined forces with Captain Michael A. Healy, of the U. S. Revenue Cutter *Bear,* who was essentially the federal government's law enforcement presence in the vast territory of Alaska. In his extensive travels Healy had witnessed the success of the Chukchi people of eastern Siberia at raising reindeer, and he suggested the idea to Jackson of transporting domestic reindeer from Siberia to western Alaska as a solution to the food shortages among Native Alaskans.

Beginning with a successful trial run of 16 reindeer imported to the Aleutian Islands in 1891, Captain Healy made five trips to Siberia during the summer of 1892 and thus began the establishment of small reindeer herds, which were distributed to mission schools on the Seward Peninsula and throughout western Alaska under the direction of Jackson.

By 1905 the reindeer population was estimated at over 10,000 animals, due in part to the discovery of gold in Nome in 1898, when a large demand for reindeer meat popularized their raising. Reindeer, who could graze freely on native lichen and did not need to be fed, were also used to pull sleds full of gear and supplies for the miners, and in 1899 reindeer were used to deliver mail for the U.S. postal service.

The first route was established by Sheldon Jackson, from St. Michael to Kotzebue, and another early route, managed by William Kjellmann, ran from the Eaton Reindeer Station, near Unalakleet, over what must have been the same route followed by today's Iditarod trail, to

Caption on this photo reads: "Sled deer hauling reindeer meat to village. Deering herd, 1928. Photographer Clarence Leroy Andrews.
Clarence Leroy Andrews Photograph Collection P45-0588 Alaska State Library

United States reindeer mail team, Nome to Teller route. Lomen Bros. photo.
Lomen Brothers Photograph Collection P28-180 Alaska State Library

Nome. The establishment of reindeer stations throughout western Alaska allowed the use of reindeer relays of from thirty to fifty miles, carrying 200-300 pounds of mail. A photo taken at Anvik Mission by Rev. J.W. Chapman shows multiple reindeer teams being readied to leave from in front of the mission with 1,023 pounds of mail bound for Kaltag.

In 1906, a government investigation found that the majority of the reindeer in Alaska were owned by mission schools and non-Natives, so Dr. Jackson's services were ended and a government policy was established with the goal of placing more reindeer into Native Alaskan ownership. The U. S. Reindeer Service was formed with reindeer distribution largely handled by school superintendents employed by the Bureau of Education, and the reindeer population grew to an estimated 20,000 head by the close of 1908. By 1913 Alaskan Natives owned over 65% of the estimated 47,266 reindeer in Alaska.

The herds grew quickly over the following twenty years and in the 1930s the reindeer population peaked at 640,000. Colorful Alaskan characters became identified with the reindeer industry, such as Carl J. Lomen, known as The Reindeer King of Alaska for his unstinting role in organizing, promoting, marketing, and lobbying for the reindeer industry; and a Native woman, Mary Antisarlook, known as Sinrock Mary the Reindeer Queen, grew famous for her immense herd of reindeer and became one of the richest women in the North.

In 1937 the Reindeer Act was passed and restricted ownership of domestic reindeer to Native Alaskans. For a complexity of reasons the herds were already in decline by that time, and by 1950 there were only 25,000 reindeer reported to be under private ownership.

Meanwhile the sled dog, which had been used as a draft animal for centuries, was gaining popular favor as a practical means of transporting goods, materials, and people over long trails under the most adverse conditions. The Klondike gold rush saw the importation of thousands of dogs to the north country from 1897 to 1899, and the Fairbanks and Nome gold rushes which quickly followed brought even more dogs to Alaska and the Yukon, cementing a legend of dauntless dogs bravely forging through blizzards, over mountains, and down rivers with their masters' loads.

When the Nome Kennel Club, founded in 1906, organized a series of races to encourage the breeding and training of better sled dogs, their place as primary transportation animals was strengthened. The 408-mile All Alaska Sweepstakes, founded in 1908, captured the imagination of an entire nation with colorful champions such as Scotty Allen and Leonhard Seppala. Their teams blazed across remote and dangerous trails, and their thrilling exploits under the northern lights were immortalized in popular novels such as Esther Birdsall Darling's *Baldy of Nome* and Barrett Willoughby's romance based on the All Alaska Sweepstakes, *The Trail Eater*.

When the Nome diphtheria epidemic struck in 1925, the use of sled dog teams in relaying the life-saving serum once again galvanized public attention and popularized the working sled dog. Leonhard Seppala and Gunnar Kaasen travelled to major cities and exhibited their serum run teams, and a bronze statue of Balto in New York's Central Park was ceremoniously unveiled by the famous leaddog himself.

Sheldon Jackson may have vociferously testified against the sled dog before Congress, but the reign of the reindeer in Alaska was relatively short-lived in the history of the north. They're still being raised in northwestern Alaska, although not in the vast numbers seen during Carl Lomen and Mary Antilarsook's time.

The Reindeer Research Program, established in 1981, has taken an active role in the re-development and promotion of the Alaskan reindeer industry, noting that currently, there are approximately 20 reindeer herders and 20,000 reindeer in western Alaska. An additional 10,000 reindeer exist in herds on Nunivak, St. Paul, Umnak, and other Aleutian Islands, along with a few fenced herds along Alaska's road system. ~•~

Reindeer King Carl J. Lomen

Sinrock Mary, Reindeer Queen

Mary Joyce with her sled dogs, ca. 1936. Photo by Harry T. Becker.
Harry T. Becker Photograph Collection P67-0246 Alaska State Library

Mary Joyce, Adventurer

Mushing from Juneau to Fairbanks

Mary Joyce was an Alaskan adventurer of the highest caliber, and when Alaska was still just a territory she owned and operated a remote lodge near Juneau, became the first woman radio operator in the territory, and flew her own bush plane. In later years, after selling her lodge, she joined Pan Alaska Airways as a stewardess, and then settled in Juneau, where she worked as a nurse and bought two popular local bars.

Mary Joyce's biggest claim to fame, besides her dauntless courage in trying new adventures, was her 1936 dogsled trip from her Taku Lodge near Juneau to Fairbanks, 1,000 miles away.

She was invited to participate in the 1936 Fairbanks Ice Carnival as a representative for the City and Borough of Juneau. Always ready for an adventure, Mary decided to drive her dogs on the thousand-mile journey. Leaving in late December for the March event, she hitched five dogs to her sled and joined a group of Natives headed for Atlin, British Columbia for the initial part of the long trip.

At Tulsequah, the party crossed the nearly frozen Taku River. Journaling as she traveled, Mary wrote about one of her trail guides: "Chocak Lagoose scolded his sons and made them put boughs over holes so I could not see the water underneath while crossing. 'White Lady plenty scared.' Crossed on my hands and knees and dogs followed like soldiers. Crossed upper Taku and another place over rapids on huge cakes of ice three feet apart helped by sweepers and snags. Put chain on Tip (lead dog) and each dog fell into water, pulled them out

Mary's leader, Wolf, was featured on a 1954 menu for the Alaska Steamship Line series, by the beloved Alaskan artist Josephine Crumrine. The caption reads: "A peerless leader of the famous team raced by Mary Joyce in the annual Alaska Dog Derby, Wolf has also made a trip to the States. He spent a season at Sun Valley, Idaho, hauling winter sports enthusiasts on a real Alaskan dog sledge."

Mary Joyce Photograph Collection
P459-491 Alaska State Library

Based on Mary's journals, this 2007 book details her adventure.

on another cake of ice. In places, just room for sled on ice cakes with water leaping over and gurgling underneath."

Mary's journey had barely begun with that adventure, and it wasn't until a week later that she reached the most hazardous part of the trip, between Burwash Landing and Tanana Crossing, where she was following the Kluane River in temperatures reaching sixty degrees below zero. A biographical note at the Alaska State Library Historical Collections explains what happened next: "The rate of her progress slowed when she became ill en route, causing the public to fear for her safety and speculate on her whereabouts. She flew to the Winter Carnival after realizing she would not complete the trek in time, but returned to her sled and completed the mush after the event.

"The route Mary traversed followed the path of what eventually became the Alaska Highway. For this effort she was awarded a Silver Cup from the city, a 2-month-old husky pup from friend Don Abel, Sr., and a rare 'Honorary Member' title from the Pioneers of Alaska. Her story attracted national media attention."

Mary kept a journal of her trip which was published in 2007 with the title, *Mary Joyce, Taku to Fairbanks, 1,000 Miles by Dogteam*, by her cousin, Mary Anne Greiner, who wrote glowingly of Mary for the back cover: "She was the first white person over a portion of the trail which later became part of the Alcan Highway. Her narrative and descriptions of Alaska's people, dogteams, vast landscapes and dangers encountered on the trail are wrapped in her wry humor and perspectives of the 30s..."

After Mary's dogsled adventure she invested and co-starred in a film that was shot on location in the Taku River region, *Orphans of the North* (1940), and in the late 1930s and early '40s she became a flight stewardess on Pan-Alaska Airlines, a subsidiary of Pan-American Airlines.

In the winter of 1939 Mary conducted sled-dog tours of the Sun Valley Resort in Idaho. During the Second World War, after warnings of an impending Japanese invasion of Alaska, she moved into the capitol city of Juneau and worked as a nurse at St. Ann's Hospital until the end of the war. After 14 years and at the conclusion of the war, Mary sold Taku Lodge and purchased the Top Hat Bar in Juneau. Later she purchased the Lucky Lady and lived in an apartment above it.

Mary Joyce ran for the office of Alaskan Territorial Representative in 1950, and was reportedly "an important and well-loved Alaskan figure who was regularly invited to speeches and ceremonies both in Alaska and in the contiguous United States. With the exception of a short stay in Wisconsin during the 1940s, she lived in Juneau the remainder of her life. In 1976 she suffered two heart attacks, the second of which took her life. She is buried at the Evergreen Cemetery in Juneau."

Mary's adventures are also described in *Women Pilots of Alaska: 37 Interviews and Profiles*, by Sandi Sumner; and *TAKU: Four Amazing Individuals-Four Incredible Life Stories and The Alaskan Wilderness Lodge That Brought Them Together*, by Karen Bell and Janet Shelfer. ~•~

Mary's team in the 4th of July parade, Juneau, 1959
"The day the 49th star was added to the flag."
Margaret A. Hreha Collection ASL-P251-I-BookB48-04

Leonhard Seppala and his huskies.
Otto Nordling Collection UAF-1974-135-1 University of Alaska Fairbanks

Olympic Sled Dogs

Mushing Luminaries Competed

Every so often, usually as the Winter Olympic competitions are once again riveting the world's attention and interest in snow-related adventures, the question arises why sled dog racing is not a recognized Olympic sport. There's no easy answer to the question, but proponents of the idea can take encouragement from history. To the surprise of many mushing enthusiasts, a sled dog race was run as a demonstration sport at the 1932 Winter Olympics in Lake Placid, New York. Held in February, it was the third Winter Olympics event, and the first one held in North America. The Games were opened by New York Governor Franklin D.

Roosevelt, who would be elected President of the United States later the same year. Basketball star Wilt Chamberlain carried the Olympic Torch.

The sled dog race, run as a demonstration of a sport indigenous to the United States and North America, was included because, as was noted in *The Official Report for the 1932 Winter Olympics*: "Winter travel by dog team in the northeastern snow belt of the United States, in Canada, and in Alaska, is both a sport and a measure of necessity when all other means of getting across the frozen wastes of snow fail. In the Far North dog teams carry mail and freight and follow regular routes and schedules."

The race was held under the rules of the New England Sled Dog Club over a 25 mile course, run each day for two days for a total of 50 miles. Five contestants from Canada and seven teams from the United States competed with seven dogs per sled, each team leaving at three minute intervals. The *Official Report* stated "Many American and Canadian sportsmen are interested in the raising or racing of sled dogs, Siberian, Alaskan, or Labrador breeds, the best racing teams usually being cross-bred. Dog derbies have for years been a picturesque part of the winter sports-life of Lake Placid, and the Olympic demonstration derby was one of the most picturesque and interesting events on the entire program."

The racers included Alaska's own celebrated 'King of the Trail,' Leonard Seppala, who had gained nationwide attention only a few years previously for his role in the lifesaving serum run to Nome. Another well-known entrant was Colonel Norman D. Vaughan, who had just returned from Antarctic exploration as a dog driver for Admiral Richaed E. Byrd. Also running the race was a woman, Eva "Short" Seeley, who was very influential in the development and recognition of the Alaskan Malemute and the Siberian Husky.

Emile St. Godard's team, 1929

Leonhard Seppala

Emile St. Godard

Emile St. Godard, a French Canadian from The Pas, Manitoba, had won The Pas Dog Derby in 1925, which was one of the world's premier sled dog races at the time. He was destined to become Canada's most revered champion musher and the only sled dog musher in Canada's Sports Hall of Fame, dominating the field for so long that fans often commented it would be "St. Godard against the field."

Alaskan Leonhard Seppala and Canadian Emile St. Godard faced each other annually at the Eastern International Dog Derby in Quebec. Over six years, St. Godard would win the race four times, and Seppala twice. They also faced off in a variety of different races over the years, of which St. Godard won the majority.

Arthur Daley, sportswriter for *The New York Times*, wrote: "Lake Placid, New York, February 8, 1932. In the colorful sled dog race it was a Canadian team that was victorious as Emile St. Godard, the veteran Manitoba musher, emerged as the victor over Leonhard Seppala of the United States… These two keen rivals, less than a minute and a half apart after the first twenty five miles yesterday, again staged a bitter battle on the second twenty five mile route today. St. Godard proved that his Russian Wolfhound-Malamutes were faster dogs when he finished first once more, compiling a total time of 4 hours, 27 minutes, 12.5 seconds. Seppala, famous for his race with death to bring the antitoxin to Nome, was clocked in at 4 hours, 31 minutes, 1.8 seconds for the fifty miles."

Following St. Godard's victory Seppala acknowledged his rival's superiority as a sled dog driver, returned to Alaska and would never compete with him again. St. Godard was inducted to Canada's Sports Hall of Fame in 1952, where his biography reads in part: "St.

Godard was known not only for his winning record, but also for his concern for the well-being of his dogs. He once withdrew from a race just after reaching the homestretch because his dogs were cutting their paws on the jagged ice that covered the trail. In the end, he preferred to relinquish a victory than cause harm to his huskies. Legend has it that his dogs derived their incredible speed and stamina from a steady diet of Lake Winnipeg Goldeye fish. Proving that they were more than just a team, St. Godard fondly referred to this canine clan as his 'family.' His lead dog, Toby, who was half-husky, half-greyhound, was such an integral part of this crew that when he was no longer fit for racing, St. Godard retired from competition. St. Godard remains the only dogsled racer to be inducted into Canada's Sports Hall of Fame."

In his landmark essay, "A History of Mushing Before We Knew It," champion musher and sled dog historian Tim White wrote: "Despite the international character of the participants in the race in Lake Placid, there was little activity outside North America except in Norway, where the use of dogs for military supply and ambulance work beginning at the time of the First World War had been transformed into a sport. The influence of Nansen and Amundsen, who used sled dogs in the North and South Polar regions, was also important in establishing a Scandinavian sled dog sport.

"In the 1952 Oslo Olympics sled dogs were featured again as a Demonstration Sport, this time in the form of pulka races where the driver accompanies the dogs on skis behind a toboggan or pulka." ~•~

Sled Dog Race, Demonstration

Driver	Country	Owner	First Race	Second Race	Total
St Goddard	Canada	St Goddard	2:12:5	2:11:7.5	4:23:12.5
Seppala	United States	Seppala	2:13:34.3	2:17:27.5	4:31:1.8
Russick	Canada	Russick	2:26:22.4	2:21:22.2	4:47:44.6
Wheeler	Canada	Wheeler	2:33:19.1	2:29:35	5:02:54.1
Haines	United States	Taylor	2:34:56	2:31:31.3	5:06:27.3
Pouliot	Canada	Marquis	2:53:14.3	2:52:21.5	5:45:39.8
Defalco	Canada	Defalco	2:53:49.5	2:55:50.1	5:49:39.6
Belknap	United States	Belknap	2:57:14	2:57:8.5	5:54:22.5
Murphy	United States	McIlhenny	2:42:49.4	3:15:24.1	5:58:13.5
Sears	United States	d'Avignon	3:21.7	3:1:49.5	6:02:11.2
Vaughan	United States	Seeley	3:24:10	3:49:46	7:13:56
Seeley (Mrs)	United States	Seeley	3:28:1.7	3:46:45	7:14:46.7

Trophies from the 1909 and 1910 All Alaska Sweepstakes races at the Carrie McLain Museum in Nome. Photo by Helen Hegener/Northern Light Media.

All Alaska Sweepstakes

World's Oldest Organized Sled Dog Race

"On a cold spring day in 1907 a group of us gathered around the stove in a Nome saloon and began talking about dog races. After a few weeks of arguing we worked out the rules of the 'All-Alaska Sweepstakes.' Beginning with the spring of 1908 this great race of dog teams was run every year until the war, the last one in 1917. It became world famous, and has set the pace for every important dog race since." -A.A. "Scotty" Alllan, *Gold, Men and Dogs* (G.P. Putnam's Sons, 1931)

The All Alaska Sweepstakes is the oldest organized sled dog race in the world, with records kept by the Nome Kennel Club dating back to the first race in 1908. The route from Nome, on the south side of the Seward Peninsula, to the small community of Candle on the north side and return, is 408 miles, following the telegraph lines which linked camps, villages and gold mining settlements on the Peninsula. This route's established communication lines allowed those betting on the outcome to track the race more easily from the comfort of saloons like the famed Board of Trade in Nome, where the Nome Kennel Club was founded the previous year.

Scotty Allan describes the trail to Candle in his classic 1931 autobiography about the Nome gold rush and his colorful racing adventures, *Gold, Men and Dogs*: "It was selected because the trail to it from Nome goes over all kinds of country, from sea ice to high mountains, with rivers, tundra, timber, glaciers, and everything else in the way of mental and physical hardships en route. We knew there wouldn't be any doubt about the excellence of a dog or driver that covered it."

In her booklet and official souvenir history of the race, titled *The Great Dog Races of Nome Held Under the Auspices of the Nome Kennel Club, Nome, Alaska*, author and 1916 Nome Kennel Club President Esther Birdsall Darling described the "why" of the race: "It was early seen that not only would the races furnish much of the winter entertainment. but that there would also be a consistent effort on the part of the dog owners and dog drivers to improve the breed of sled dogs, which up to this time had been but little considered; an effort to instill into all dog

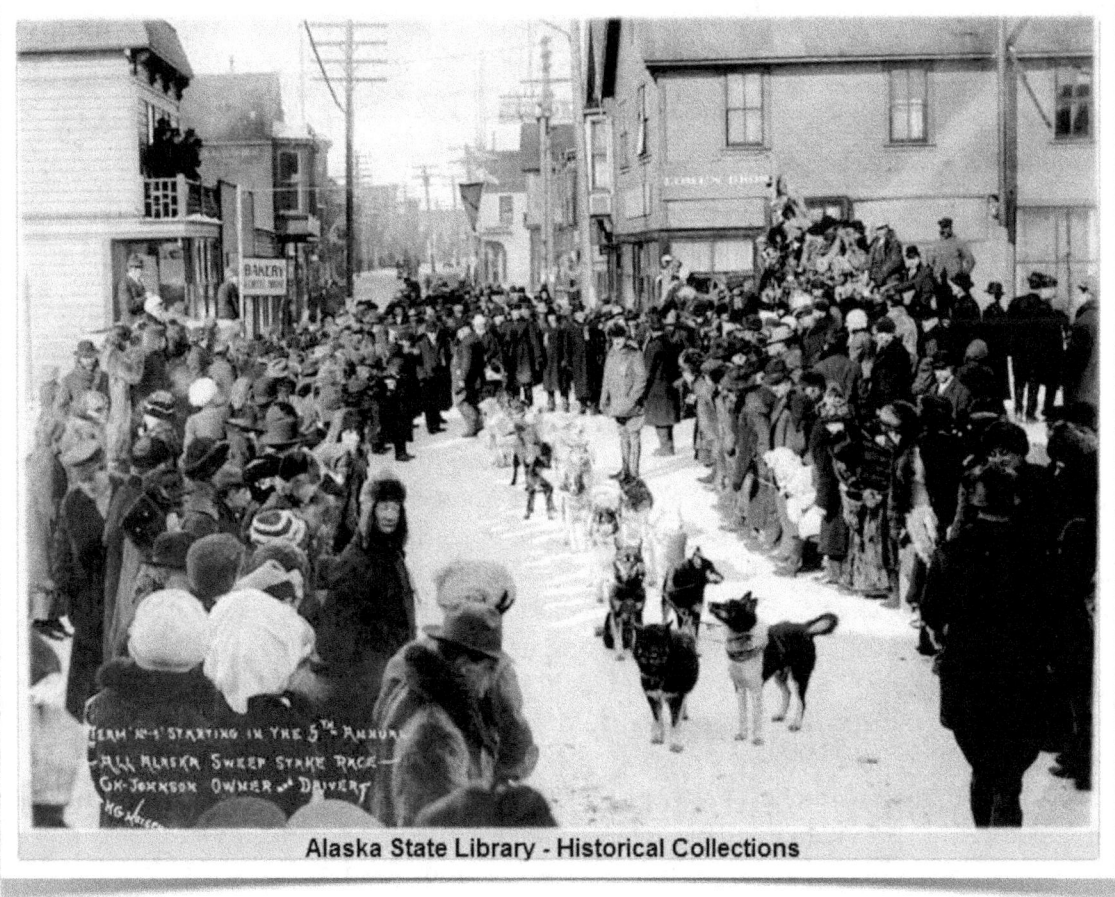

Team No. 1 starting the 5th All Alaska Sweepstakes, April 4, 1912.
G.H. Johnson, owner/driver. Photo by H.G. Kaiser.
Dr. Daniel S. Neuman Photographs P307-0313 AK St Library

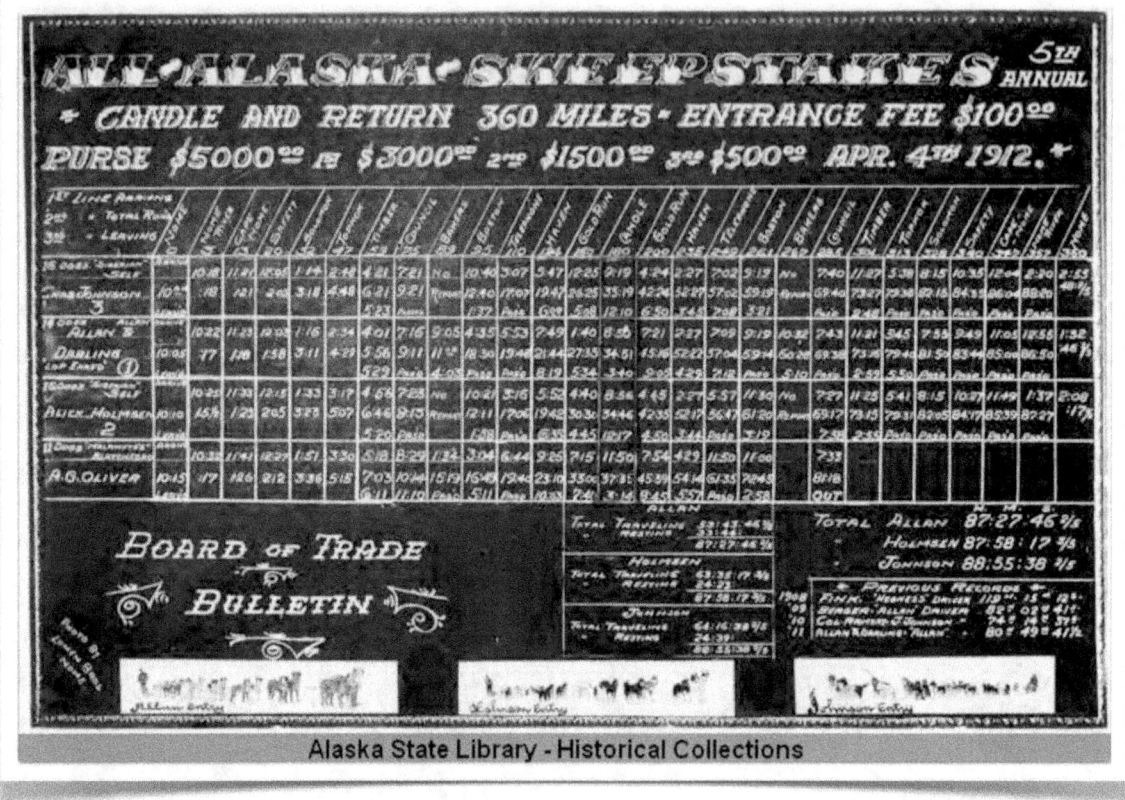

5th Annual All Alaska Sweepstakes, Nome to Candle and return, 360 miles.
Dr. Daniel S. Neuman Photograph Collection P307-0317 Alaska State Library

users an intelligent understanding of the accepted fact that care and kindness to their dogs bring the quickest and surest returns from all standpoints. This has resulted in the development of such a high standard for dogs that not alone is their worth acknowledged throughout Alaska, but their supremacy is conceded the world over."

One of the race's most popular dog drivers was a likable Scotsman named Allan Alexander Allan, known as Scotty. Perhaps the most famous musher of his time, Scotty Allan had prospected in the Klondike, following adventure trails from there to Nome, where he quickly joined forces with the aforementioned Esther Birdsall Darling to create the Allan and Darling kennel, historically one of the best known racing kennels in Alaska.

Scotty Allan's venerable leader was a dog named Baldy, and he led Allen to first place in 1909, 1911 and 1912, and to a career total of eight top-three finishes in the race. Baldy's exploits were memorialized in a best-selling children's book by Allan's kennel co-owner, Esther Birdsall Darling, titled *Baldy of Nome* and published in 1913. Veteran race judge Al Crane declared the book 'must reading' for anyone seeking to understand the All Alaska Sweepstakes.

Scotty Allan provided dogs for the U.S. government during World War I to haul supplies over the mountains from France to Germany, and his leader Navarre, a grandson of Baldy and also featured in a book by Esther Birdsall Darling, was awarded the French Cross for his heroic duty. Scotty Allan later went on to become a well-respected representative in the Territorial Legislature of Alaska.

Interpretive signs in the Carrie McLain Museum in Nome tell interesting details of the famous race: "At the checkpoints along the trail, handlers aided the drivers with the dogs so they could rest. During the short stops the dogs were given Eagle canned milk which is easily digested and nourishing. Every hundred miles, the teams took a five or six hour rest, and the dogs would be fed raw ptarmigan or ground raw mutton. The drivers wore regulation mushing clothes: an everyday parka, a light fur parka, a stocking cap and a fur cap, plenty of canvas gloves and heavy fur mitts. They used light racing sleds built with hoops instead of straight handles at the back. The hoop was easier to hold onto when riding the runners, and there was less chance of losing your grip and your team."

With colorful drivers like Scotty Allan and Leonhard Seppala, who also won the race three times (1915-1917), the All Alaska Sweepstakes was an eagerly anticipated annual event until the First World War interrupted everything. After the war gold mining dropped off and Nome's population dwindled, along with the local interest in sled dog racing. Finally, in 1983, after several years of planning and preparation, and with the boost in interest brought about by the then-famous Iditarod Trail Sled Dog Race, the Nome Kennel Club was able to bring back the All Alaska Sweepstakes for the 75th Anniversary of the race. Rick Swenson won that year, taking home the $25,000.00 winner-take-all purse.

Twenty-five years later, in 2008, the 100th Anniversary of the event saw the Nome Kennel Club offer the richest purse ever raised for a sled dog race: $100,000.00 winner-take-all! Sixteen teams entered, with mushers from all across Alaska hoping to have their name engraved on the trophy beside racing legends Scotty Allan and Leonhard Seppala. In total, only four mushers besides Allan and Seppala had ever won the race: John Hegness in 1908, John "Iron Man" Johnson in 1910 and 1914, Fay Dalzene in 1913 and Rick Swenson in 2008.

The 1910 time set by "Iron Man" Johnson, driving a team of Siberian huskies which had been imported by Fox Maule Ramsay, had never been broken. He ran the 408-mile trail in 74 hours, 14 minutes, and 37 seconds. For many years Scotty Allan and Leonhard Seppala tried to break "Iron Man" Johnson's record-setting run, but could never do so.

The entrants for the Centennial running in 2008 were formidable and included the 1983 champion, Rick Swenson, who had also won the 1,000-mile Iditarod five times, more than any other musher. Competitors for the one hundred thousand dollar purse also included four-time Iditarod champion Jeff King, 2004 Iditarod champion Mitch Seavey, the reigning Iditarod champion Lance Mackey at the top of his game, and several other mushers who were often at or near the top in mid- and long-distance races. The race was run according to the original race rules, which differed in many aspects from the races of the day, such as every dog must be brought back to the starting line (no dropped dogs), and handlers could assist the teams on the trail.

The 2004 Iditarod champion, Mitch Seavey, won the race, and his time, along with the times of fellow Iditarod champions Jeff King and Lance Mackey, who came in second and third respectively, finally broke the 75-year-old record set by "Iron Man" Johnson in 1910.

When the 1983 race champion Rick Swenson was asked how he rated the All Alaska Sweepstakes, he reputedly replied; "It's a historic event, and on a scale of 1 to 10 it's probably an 11. It's an 11 on historical significance, it's an 11 on its difficulty to finish, and it takes an 11 in dog care to win." ~•~

Ghosts of the Trail

Running with Spirits

There are strange things done
'neath the midnight sun
By the men who moil for gold.
The arctic trails have their secret tales
That would make your blood run cold.
  -Robert Service, *The Cremation of Sam McGee*

There's a 1988 print by official Iditarod artist Jon Van Zyle titled "Beyond the Unknown," and it represents Van Zyle's encounter with spirits on the Yukon River. Van Zyle tells the story behind his painting in Lew Freedman's book, *Iditarod Classics*, how he was mushing along the Yukon River between Blackburn and Kaltag around three or four in the morning, and then, "As I got closer to this area, I heard 'whisper, whisper, whisper' - talking. A murmuring. And it got louder and louder and more distinct. That went into laughter. Nothing raucous, not 'Ho, ho, ho' - just nice laughter. Like someone was having a good time..."

Van Zyle explained how the laughter alternated with applause which would get loud and then taper off, and he continued, "Nobody was there. I wasn't dreaming, I was awake. When I came back I did a painting about it. A priest called. He said, 'I used to be on the Yukon River and I know where that spot is.'"

Van Zyle never met the priest, but he did some research and learned there was a massacre in the area, some missionaries were killed, and he wrote, "I think those are the people. They were watching a bunch of crazy dog mushers. And they gave me a little round of applause. I think it was neat. The priest told me, 'You're not the first person who's heard these people.'"

When the Iditarod Trail Sled Dog Race takes the southern route it passes the ghost town of Iditarod, and it's a notoriously spooky place. Author and musher Don Bowers, who was killed in the crash of his small plane in 2000, compiled detailed notes on the Iditarod Trail, and they're still an excellent reference for anyone interested in knowing what's out there. His entry on the section of trail from Ophir to Iditarod warns, "Even with the bustle of the checkpoint, this is still a lonely, haunted place. It's hard to believe there were 10,000 people here in 1910, and the town had electricity, telephones, newspapers, banks, and hotels. Fortunes were made and lost here, and legends about the boom days could fill entire books. All that is ancient history, and the wilderness has reclaimed almost everything.

"Wolves howl at night amid the old collapsed buildings, reminding you that this is their territory now. The only things that are about the same as in 1910 are the unending snow and cold, the Big Dipper swinging silently around the North Star amid the northern lights—and your dog team."

In an article on the 2009 race, *Anchorage Daily News* reporter Kevin Klott told the story of musher John Rickert, who was spending the night in a cabin in the now-abandoned gold rush town of Ophir. He saw and talked with someone messing with the wood-burning stove in the

Yukon Quest team running at night, 2008. Northern Light Media photo.

middle of the night, but in the morning learned there'd been no one there. "'I saw something, someone,' Rickert was still insisting days later..."

For an October, 2011 article for *Alaska Dispatch* titled *Ghosts of Alaska's Iditarod Trail*, Jill Burke wrote about an encounter which respected veteran musher DeeDee Jonrowe related when she pulled into Iditarod: "'When I came there in the early years, I was certain I saw other teams,' Jonrowe says. 'But they were old teams, wrapped in blankets and wolf skins.'

"Jonrowe questions whether her haunting vision was merely a trick of the mind. But she has a hard time dismissing the smoky smell from the bygone miners' fires. 'All of those people are there, and you can see and hear and smell the wood smoke,' she recalls. The ghost town clattered with the noise of fire pokes and slamming doors as miners milled around, their arms heavy with gold weights and scales. 'They weren't happy to see you. They would just give you looks like they were hoarding their stuff,' Jonrowe recalls. 'You wanted to get away from them.'"

After leaving Iditarod there's an eerie quality to the trail between Iditarod and Shageluk. Don Bowers' *Trail Notes* advise: "There is absolutely no human habitation for the entire route—no cabins, no mines, nothing. The people of Shageluk rarely have any need to go over to Iditarod and Flat and vice versa, so this trail is normally only put in every other year, and then only for the Iditarod. Much of the area between Iditarod and Shageluk was burned in a forest fire years ago and some areas still have not grown back. In short, it will be pretty lonely and maybe even a little spooky. This is a good leg to find another driver to run with, just for the company if nothing else."

Just as the Iditarod trail leaves the protection of the inland woods and hills and heads for the open and exposed Bering Sea coastline beyond Unalakleet, there's a well-known landmark which gives many mushers pause, a place long known among the racers for its still-wandering spirits. In his log of the Iditarod Trail between Kaltag and Unalakleet, Don Bowers described Old Woman Cabin: "The trail will swing off the sloughs and into the trees, where you'll see an old plywood cabin. This is the original Old Woman cabin... If you stop here, make sure you leave something (such as food) for the Old Woman when you leave. You don't want her ghost chasing you to Nome and throwing bad luck your way."

Jill Burke included Jonrowe's experiences at Old Woman in her article: "There's something about the mountain and the old cabin -- which, legend has it, belonged to a woman who once lived there and may never have left -- that infiltrates a musher's desires. It's happened to Jonrowe at least a half-dozen times. Old Woman 'kind of hums,' she says. 'First you think the humming is the wind coming through the boards. But it's a tune, soothing but also kind of haunting, with minor notes rather than melodious notes.' Like a siren calling out to sea-weary sailors, Old Woman's power is in her ability to hold mushers suspended in time. One time I spent nearly 24 hours there,' Jonrowe says. 'She is a time-suck. You just want to rest for a bit, but you stay longer. She definitely can wreck the strategy of a race.'"

Another musher who's tangled with the spirits at Old Woman is Doug Katchatag of Unalakleet. He was running a local race near there as night fell and suddenly his dog team slowed and then refused to move. He could see the hair standing on end on his dogs, and when he finally got them moving again a figure appeared from nowhere and grabbed his shoulders. He yelled at the apparition and it disappeared. Jill Burke's article relates another incident: "Katchatag says he heard of another strange encounter when a local family was visiting Old Woman. When a boy in the group was exploring the cabin's attic, he saw a beautiful woman. Entranced by the woman, the child had to be pulled off the steps to the attic. The incident was so haunting that the rest of the family refused to check out the second level of the cabin. 'If a little boy like that could see a ghost, then you know there are ghosts,' Katchatag says."

In her 1998 book *Iditarod Country*, Tricia Brown shared a story from then-City Manager of Elim, Luther Nagaruk: "We have some ghosts between here and Koyuk. These are lights. Usually if you're going too far out on the ice, these lights come on along the coast. I've seen it myself. The Iditarod dog mushers have seen them, too. Mostly near the old settlements along the coast. Strange things happen. Never to hurt anybody; mostly to help people. I know one musher that was coming along here one time. He stopped against a fence, he thought it was a graveyard. He camped there and when he woke up the next morning, there was no fence there."

In his autobiography, *The Lance Mackey Story*, the four-time Iditarod champion shares his own tale of the trail, which happened on the Yukon River, not far from Anvik, in the 2009 race: "It's common to squint your eyes when you're tired, and I've seen things on the ice like a drift log that looks like a boat, light tracers, or ice that looks like an animal. This time, I saw a woman ahead of me. She was sitting beside the trail and not really doing anything except staring at me. The closer I got, the more real she was, and when I passed, she smiled. But when I turned around to wave good-bye, she was gone. I felt I was really awake and had no doubt she was there. It was such a strange experience that it rattled me."

In his 2010 book titled *Yukon Quest* Lew Freedman writes of musher Bruce Lee's trail hallucinations: "Frequently he heard things. Lee had complete conversations with people who were not present on the trail. It kept happening until he almost drove himself nuts. Other times mushing through the night he would hear his name called. 'Hey, Bruce!' someone would shout. 'Of course there was nobody there. I was in the middle of the Yukon River.'" ~•~

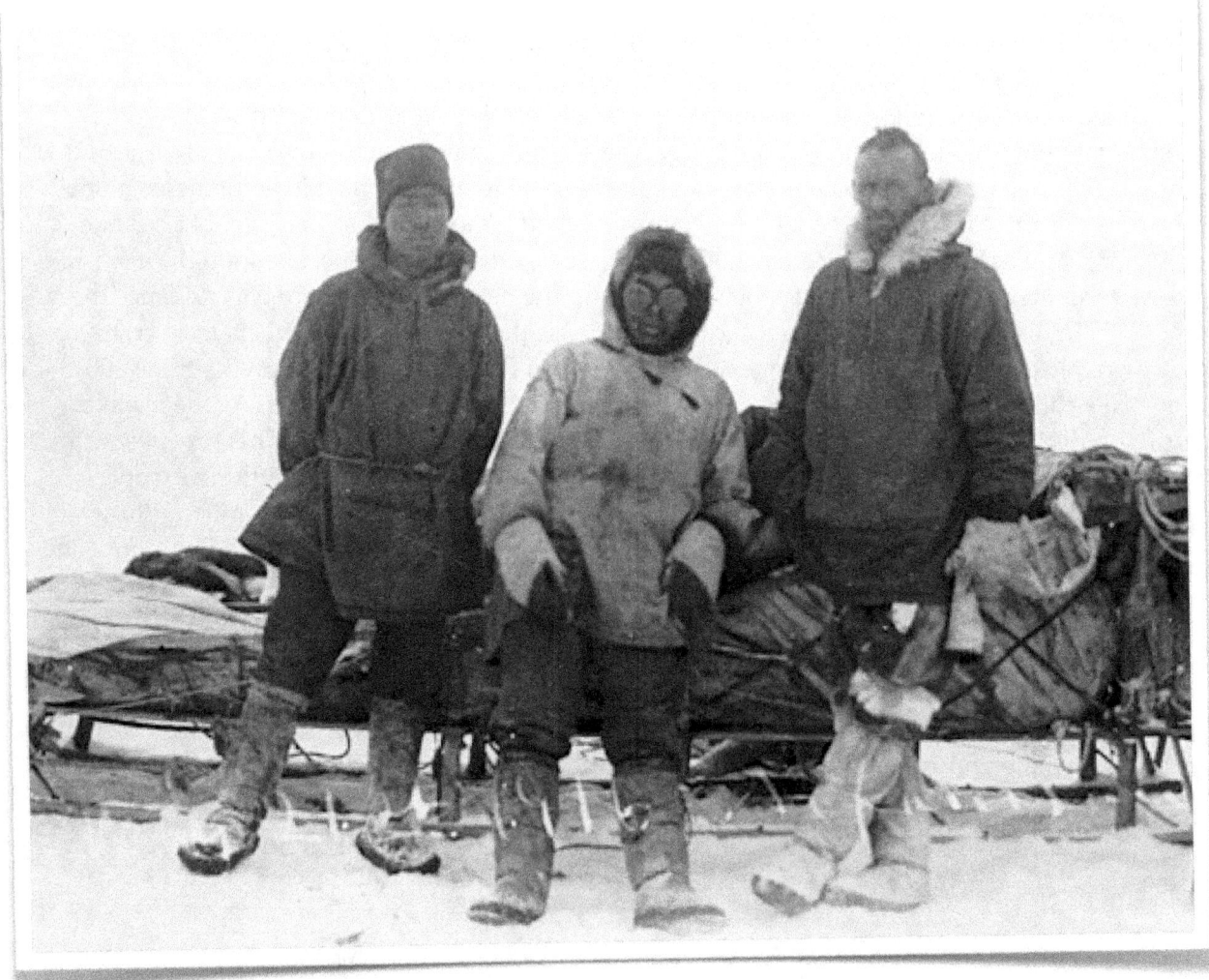

Natkusiak, Emiu and Karsten Andersen in front of a long expedition sled, Borden Island, Northwest Territories, Canada. Photo by Vilhjalmur Stefansson, May, 1916

Split-the-Wind

"...the greatest musher..."

The Canadian Arctic Expedition, organized in July, 1913 under the leadership of explorer and anthropologist Vilhjalmur Stefansson, was designed to be the most comprehensive scientific study of the Arctic ever attempted, comprised of a multi-pronged approach to researching and documenting the most northerly reaches of the North American continent.

Scientists of many disciplines, and from several countries, answered the call and joined the expedition, and while many of them lost their lives, most returned almost four years later with thousands of artifacts, specimens, photos, film and sound recordings; scientific data and knowledge which has been used in Arctic science ever since.

Unfortunately in the winter of 1913 the expedition met with fiercer than normal weather, and all of the expedition ships were frozen into the ice before they could reach their initial destination of Herschel Island. The *Karluk*, the flagship of the expedition, was eventually crushed by the ice, leading to loss of eleven lives before a famous rescue by the revenue cutter *Bear*.

One of the most compelling books to come out of the Canadian Arctic Expedition was written by Harold Noice, who joined as a sailor and crew member on the schooner *Polar Bear* when she left Seattle in March 1915. Noice maintained a detailed diary during his time with Stefansson's exploration party, and was with the intrepid explorer during the discovery of new lands in 1916 and 1917.

In 1924 Harold Noice published an account of his adventures with the Canadian Arctic Expedition, titled *With Stefansson in the Arctic*. In his book, Noice told of an Eskimo guide for Vilhjalmer Stefannsson's expeditions named Emiu, who was also known as "Split-the-wind" due to his fondness for fast dogteams.

Originally from Nome, and formerly a cabin boy on the schooner *Polar Bear*, Emiu took part in all of the 'New Land' sled trips in the Arctic islands between 1916 and 1918. Emiu had, according to Noice, spent two years in Seattle and most of the rest of his life in Nome, Alaska.

Arctic explorer Viljhalmur Stefansson and his fellow expedition members took thousands of photographs of their travels in the Arctic. March, 1914.

Emiu, known as Split-the-Wind

Schooner Polar Bear

"Split was a game little fellow, like a compact bundle of fine steel wires. He had a habit of pulling his belt tight which made him look even more gaunt than he was, and at camp-time he used to delight in talking about the fine beefsteaks we would order when we finally got back to civilization."

"Split told us… how on such a date he had trained the team of racing dogs that won the All Alaska Sweepstakes in so many hours, 'Twenty-three minutes and eighty-nine seconds flat!'" A search of the All Alaska Sweepstakes race results for the early years of the race does not show a team finishing within that specific time configuration, and the available finishes do not include a time for 24 minutes and 29 seconds, which is what the adjusted time would be.

Split was one of several former members of the Canadian Arctic Expedition who succumbed to the influenza epidemic of 1918. According to Noice "Little Split died of influenza a few days after he reached Nome."

For the most part, Split-the-Wind has all but disappeared from the annals of history; references to the speedy little musher are difficult to find, and photos of him are rare. Unfortunately this was not an unusual development in early Alaska, when photographers needed to be selective about how they utilized photographic equipment and materials which were difficult to move and to use in the extreme northern weather conditions.

A passing mention of Split-the-Wind is found at the Iditarod Historic Trail Alliance site, as one of an elite group of Alaskan mushers: "An assortment of travelers used the Trail. The majority were prospectors, trappers, or Natives who traveled—often without dogs or with one or two to help pull a sledload of supplies—to isolated cabins. A surprising number walked along the Trail. The hero of the Trail, however, was the dogsled team and driver.

"These noteworthies earned nicknames befitting the men who raced along the Trail carrying fresh eggs or oranges, mail or express, or shipments of gold—Frank Tondreau, known from Belfast to Point Barrow as the Malemute Kid; the famous racer John "Iron Man" Johnson and his indefatigable Siberians; Captain Ulysses Grant Norton, the tireless Trojan of the trails; the Eskimo, Split-the-Wind; and the wandering Japanese, Jujira Wada. All were welcomed in the camps and became often interviewed celebrities."

There's another brief mention of this remarkable musher in the book *America's Forgotten Pandemic: the Influenza of 1918* by Alfred W. Crosby, who is Professor Emeritus in American Studies, History and Geography at the University of Texas at Austin. Crosby explains that between August, 1918 and March, 1919 the Spanish influenza spread worldwide, claiming between 50 and 130 million lives, making it one of the deadliest natural disasters in human history. In a strange twist, nearly half of those affected by the disease were healthy young adults between the ages of 20 and 40, and as the pandemic spread through the Eskimo communities around Nome it had devastating results.

Of the intrepid Emiu, Crosby writes: "One Eskimo who died was a twenty-five-year-old named Split-the-Wind, known as the greatest musher that Alaska had ever produced. He had survived incredible hardships while guiding Vilhjalmer Stefannsson, the great explorer, in the deep Arctic, eating snowshoe lacings when there was nothing better; but now he was dead of Spanish influenza, along with 750 other Eskimos of the Seward Peninsula." ~•~

Dog sleds of the Stefannson-Anderson Canadian-Arctic Expedition,
built in Nome, Alaska, 1918. Lomen Bros. photograph.

WWII sled dog patrol and rescue team

Military Sled Dogs

They Received the Croix de Guerre

When Joe Redington needed assistance relocating and marking the historic but long-forgotten Iditarod Trail in 1972, in preparation for the epic race he'd envisioned and was working to make a reality, he turned to the U.S. Army and forged a cooperative venture in which the Army helped put in the trail while gaining valuable wintertime maneuvers for their troops. Redington's history with the military had long been established: he'd spent many years doing contractual recovery work on military flights which had crashed in the remote reaches of the Alaskan back country. It must have been a bizarre sight when Joe and a team of huskies were going down the trail with a wing or the fuselage of an aircraft lashed to his dogsled.

In her book about Joe Redington, *Champion of Alaskan Huskies*, Katie Mangelsdorf wrote of Joe's work for the military with his sled dog team: "Joe's job with Rescue and Reclamation took him around the territory for seven years, and later he contracted out for specific jobs. He was called whenever a plane went down. His job was to go out and rescue the survivors or bring back their remains and then recover the downed plane. Anything not of value had to be destroyed or buried. This was so that old wreckage sites would not be reported as new crash sites." And later she noted, "Joe also freighted materials and supplies for the Air Force to White Alice sites, U.S. Air Force telecommunications sites which dotted Alaska during the Cold War."

Joe Redington's use of sled dogs in service to the military was not the first time huskies had been pressed into action for the Army in Alaska. In 1901 a young Army lieutenant named Billy Mitchell was sent to Alaska to supervise work on the Washington to Alaska Military Cable and Telegraph System. He developed a plan to use dogteams to move needed supplies and equipment into place during the winter, when the ground was frozen, in preparation for work during the long summer seasons.

Mitchell purchased the sled dogs and maintained them year-round instead of simply hiring seasonal contractors with teams; he reportedly kept two hundred dogs, running loose in a huge pack, in a large corral at Fort Egbert, near the present-day village of Eagle. Mitchell, who would later become known as the father of the U.S. Air Force, learned to drive his own team, employing the dog handling techniques of the indigenous peoples, and he used dog teams to scout the route of the telegraph line. With the assistance of the sled dog teams Mitchell's workers finished the project three years ahead of the allotted five-year schedule.

All Alaska Sweepstakes legend A.A. Scotty Allan, winner of the 1909, 1911, and 1912 races, was so well-known and his dogs so respected that when the United States entered World War I the government commissioned dogs from the Allan and Darling Kennel. Allan selected over 100 dogs from the Nome area, and trained 450 sled dogs for the French military, and they saw service hauling supplies over the Vosges Mountains between France and Germany during the severe winter of 1914-1915. Scotty Allan's famous leader, Baldy of Nome, saw 28 of his offspring enter the service and go off to war.

Allan's teams reportedly delivered over 90 tons of ammunition to an artillery battery in only four days, a feat which had previously taken up to two weeks for horses and mule teams to accomplish. It was said that two seven-dog teams could do the work of five horses in the formidable terrain. In the March, 1919 issue of *The National Geographic Magazine*, in an article titled "Mankind's Best Friend," by Ernest Harold Baynes, the details of the sled dogs' heroic

Army training of the dogs for Air-Sea rescue operations

Col. Norman D. Vaughn, veteran of Byrd's Antarctic Expedition, brought sled dogs into France during WWII

Billy Mitchell, U.S. Army, maintained over 200 sled dogs at Fort Egbert, near Eagle, on the Yukon River

actions were explained: "In four days after a very heavy snowfall, one kennel of 150 dogs moved more than 50 tons of food and supplies from the valley below to the front line on the mountain above. In the Vosges Mountains more than a thousand Alaskan sled dogs helped to hold the Hun during the last year of the war."

The article continued, referring to Esther Birdsall Darling: "One woman brought back to America a Croix de Guerre awarded by France to her intrepid teams of sled dogs. The occasion that won them that honor was their salvation of a storm-bound, foe-pressed outpost in the French Alps. Dispatch bearers had been sent out repeatedly, but no succoring answer came, for the messengers were overwhelmed as they passed through the blinding blizzard.

"At last matters became desperate. The foe was pressing his advantage with dash and courage, and nothing but quick action could save the situation. So Lieutenant Rene Haas hitched his dogs to a light sled and started through a blizzard before which human flesh, in spite of the 'urge' of a consecrated patriotism, had failed. In 'Sweepstakes racing time' they covered the trip down the mountain over and over a perilous pass to the main army post.

"There the 28 dogs were hitched to 14 light sleds, and these were loaded with ammunition. Back over the forbidding trail they went, under an artillery fire, facing a bitter wind, and plowing through blinding clouds of snow. On the fifth day, at sunrise, the panting Malamutes reached the outpost, their burden of ammunition was rushed to the gunners, and the mountain was saved from the insolent foe."

Norman Vaughan, an American sled dog driver and explorer who participated in Admiral Byrd's first expedition to the South Pole, was employed by the U.S. Army Air Forces Search and Rescue Division as a dogsled driver during WWII, engaging in many rescue missions in Greenland and attaining the rank of colonel. Charles L. Dean recounts this history in his book, *Soldiers and Sled Dogs: A History of Military Dog Mushing*.

"Hundreds of sled dogs were pressed into duty during WWII for search and rescue missions throughout Greenland, Canada and Alaska. But they also saw duty on the Western Front in one of the least-known stories of sled dog heroics that involved one of the most amazing adventurers Wintergreen has ever had the honor of being associated with. In December 1944 the German Army was making it's last stand, rolling across France and overwhelming American regiments in its path. Panzer troops drove on through bitter cold and heavy snow that rivaled the Arctic. When at last their drive was stopped by the bloody fight called the Battle of the Bulge, snows were hip deep. Motor ambulances found it impossible to rescue injured soldiers and many of the wounded lay dying in the drifts.

"Colonel Norman Vaughan sent out a rush call for dog teams. From throughout the Arctic, 209 dogs and their drivers were flown to France. Meanwhile, Vaughan experimented with the only option to get dogs to the battle front: parachutes. His superiors nixed the plan and it wasn't until Gen. Patton himself intervened that Vaughan was given the go ahead.

"By then clearing weather kept the plan from being fully deployed, but the operation had set a remarkable record and contributed to the lore of the war dogs. In fact, throughout the war, sled dogs were credited with retrieving 150 survivors, 300 casualties and millions of dollars worth of equipment."

In a review of Dean's book, Robert Kollar, an ex-scout-dog handler in the Vietnam War, succinctly describes the wartime involvement of dog teams: "During the Second World War America supplied equipment to Soviet and European allies via air routes over Alaska and the Bering Sea to Siberia and over Maine, Greenland and Labrador to Britain and later France. Search and rescue teams were vital when aircrews were forced down by extreme weather conditions in remote and harsh terrain. Survivors, casualties, and vital equipment had to be recovered and, in the days before helicopters, sled dogs were the only means available. It is estimated that 150 survivors, 300 casualties and millions of dollars of equipment were recovered. Sled dogs continued to be used by the Air Force after World War II for search and rescue until the mid-1950s when the helicopter finally closed the door.

"Sled dogs were also organized for combat. The 10th Mountain Division was created and trained for a proposed invasion of Norway. As part of the planning, the 10th became the only army division to have a sled dog unit attached, the purpose of which was to bring in supplies and bring out casualties. The proposed invasion never occurred, and the sled dogs were no longer needed and were detached from the 10th. During the Battle of the Bulge, sled dog units came close to being sent in, but bureaucratic bungling kept the mission from going forward until snows melted and it was too late.

"Both of these tasks led to an expansion in the number and organization of military sled dogs. The Army had to develop doctrine, purchase dogs, design, construct, and test sleds, and train handlers."

According to Michael G. Lemish in his book, *War Dogs: A History of Loyalty and Heroism*, when the United States entered into WWII in December, 1941, the US Army had in effect only about 50 sled dog teams, based in Alaska and used for search and rescue, and transporting equipment, supplies, ammunition, and guns. By the end of WWII, there were over 200 active military sled dog teams available, and the three northern breeds, Siberian Huskies, Alaskan Malamutes, and Alaskan Huskies, had been identified as three of only seven breeds deemed suitable for combat due to their intelligence and agility.   ~•~

Leffingwell with dogs at Flaxman Island, Canning District, Northern Alaska, ca 1910

Ernest de Koven Leffingwell

Mapping Alaska's Arctic Coastline

Ernest de Koven Leffingwell was a joint commander, with Ejnar Mikkelsen, of the 1906-1908 Anglo-American Polar Expedition, which established that, contrary to long-held myths and stories, there was no land north of Alaska.

Self-described as "the forgotten explorer," as his efforts went largely unrecognized in his own time, Leffingwell is credited for later mapping about 150 miles of the Arctic coastline, between Point Barrow and Herschel Island, along with the adjacent Brooks Range, between 1906 and 1914.

Leffingwell, Mikkelsen, and the members of their expedition became stranded on the coast of the Arctic Ocean when their schooner, the Duchess of Bedford, became ice-locked near Flaxman Island, 250 miles east of Pt. Barrow, the northernmost point of Alaska. While Leffingwell, Mikkelsen, and the ship's physician, Dr. G.P. Howe, were exploring the coastline in March and April, 1907, the sailors in the expedition used wood from their badly-damaged ship to build a rough but serviceable cabin and other structures on Flaxman Island. For the next several years, Leffingwell stayed at the camp intermittently and conducted mapping projects with Inupiat guides, traveling by dog team in the winter and following the coastline in a small boat during the summer months

Leffingwell's cabin and several other buildings on Flaxman Island still stand, and a sign was placed on them in 1971 by geologist C. G. Mull for the Alaska Division of Parks which states: "From this base camp geologist Ernest D.K. Leffingwell almost singlehandedly mapped Alaska's Arctic coast during the years 1907-1914. He also identified the Sadlerochit - main reservoir of the Prudhoe Bay field." In 1978 Leffingwell's camp was listed as a National Historic Landmark.

Leffingwell's writings include many original journals and related papers from his expeditions. In 1909 he contributed to a book, *Conquering the Arctic Ice*, authored by his friend and expedition co-commander, Ejnar Mikkelsen (Philadelphia: G. W. Jacobs); in 1915 he wrote an article, "A Communication from Leffingwell," for the *University of Chicago Magazine*; and in 1919 he authored a 247-page Professional Paper on the Canning River Region for the U.S. Geological Survey.

Ernest de Koven Leffingwell, Captain Eijnar Mikkelsen, and Dr. G.P. Howe, February, 1907, Anglo-American Polar Expedition, Canning District, Alaska

Ernest de Koven Leffingwell

Leffingwell with cases of malted milk

In *Conquering the Arctic Ice* Mikkelsen described buying dogs for the two-month exploratory expedition which he, Leffingwell, and Dr. Howe undertook in the spring of 1907: "Another serious question to be settled was that of the dogs, as several more of our pack had died, and some of those we had bought were useless. We had to get more and were willing to pay any price for them. We began at once to look about us for dogs in the possession of the Eskimos which we knew would stand us in good stead for the ones lost, but we had to pay exorbitant prices for them. For example, one which we bought from Kanara was paid for with two sacks of flour, 25 lbs. beans, 6 lbs. coffee, 20 lbs. dried potatoes, 12 lbs. cocoa, one shot-gun, 250 rounds of ammunition, and one broken-down tent; and another bought from Uxra with two sacks of flour, one sack of cornmeal, 5 lbs. coffee, 20 lbs. dried potatoes, 25 lbs. sugar, 4 lbs. prunes, 4 lbs. malted milk, 200 rounds of cartridges, and one hatchet file. The prices, as said above, were exorbitant, but the dogs were good, and what was more, we needed them."

Joe Henderson is a dog musher and arctic traveler who has explored the remote regions of Alaska over the past 30 years with his intrepid team of twenty-two Alaskan Malamutes. During the winters of 2006-2008, Joe and his Malamutes made a series of unprecedented solo expeditions in the Brooks Range and the Arctic National Wildlife Refuge. Pulling three sleds in tandem with two tons of supplies, Joe and the team mushed entirely unsupported for up to five months at a time without seeing another human being.

Henderson's expedition was a tribute to the "forgotten explorer," Ernest de Koven Leffingwell. Traveling with Leffingwell's journals as a guide, Joe covered much of the same country, camped in many of the same localities, and experienced some of the same weather and ground conditions that Leffingwell had a century before. On the third year of the expedition, Joe found Leffingwell's cabin during a whiteout blizzard.

Joe kept a detailed journal of his travels, and he wrote a three-part series of articles for *Mushing* magazine which appeared in three issues from 2006 to 2008. An excerpt: "It always amazes me how much ground Leffingwell covered. Leffingwell, along with some local Inupiat assistants, had spent six winters and nine summers surveying, mapping and studying Alaska's arctic environment. He traveled by dogteam or small boat over 4,500 miles, drew a sketch map of the entire coast between Point Barrow and the Canadian border, triangulated 150 miles of coast, and mapped the geographic features of 4,000 square miles of mainland. He also named several geologic formations, including the one that is the source of oil at the Prudhoe Bay oilfield. He journeyed 20,000 miles by ship, and he mentioned pitching camp 380 times! These are just a few of his extraordinary accomplishments." [Joe Henderson, *Retracing Leffingwell*, *Mushing Magazine*, Nov/Dec, 2008]

Leffingwell's winter quarters, Flaxman Island, Canning District, 1910

Ernest de Koven Leffingwell was awarded the Patron's Medal by the Royal Geographical Society and the Charles P. Daly Medal by the American Geographical Society, both in 1922. He was awarded an honorary Doctor of Science degree by Trinity College in 1923. Leffingwell Fork, a stream on Alaska's North Slope, Leffingwell Crags in Canada's Northwest Territories, and Leffingwell Nunatak in Greenland are named for him. When he died in 1971, he was believed to have been the oldest surviving polar explorer.   ~•~

While his trip was sponsored by The International Highway Association of Alaska and the Yukon Territory, Williams still sold postcards such as this along his route.
Slim Williams Papers, UAF-207-59-17 University of Alaska Fairbanks

Alaska Highway Trailblazer

"...blue eyes that looked miles away..."

Clyde "Slim" Williams arrived in Alaska in 1900 at the age of 18 and spent the next thirty years trapping, hunting, and blazing trails throughout the frontier. In the early 1930's Williams became a strong proponent of the plan for a highway linking Alaska to the lower 48 states, and he boasted that he could drive his dog team along the proposed route and continue all the way to Chicago, Illinois, where the 1933 Century of Progress Exposition was planned as part of the World's Fair, celebrating man's innovations in architecture, science, technology and transportation. The Alaska Road Commissioner, Donald MacDonald, persuaded Williams that such a trip could be used to promote the building of an Alaska highway, and so in 1933 Slim traveled down the proposed route by dogsled, using only crude maps in what was previously unmapped territory.

An article for the *Uniontown News Standard* reported on December 11, 1933, "He started from Copper Center, November 20, 1932, without stove, tent or compass and with only the stars, the trees and the sun to guide him. His route carried him through Dawson City, White Horse, Atlin and Telegraph Creek and after covering 1800 miles through the wildest sections of Alaska and British Columbia he reached civilization at Hazelton, B.C. On sections of this trip he traveled as far as 500 miles without seeing one human being. Cooking over an open fire and sleeping in his sled were part of the journey which was tinged with tragedy when the wolves along Forty Mile river killed one of his favorite dogs."

It took Williams five months to reach the end of the then-existing highway system near Hazelton, British Columbia. When spring thawing made sledding impossible, he mounted four Model T Ford wheels on his dogsled in Smithers, B.C. and continued toward the Chicago World's Fair. By the time he reached Seattle, Williams and his wolf-dog team had become celebrities. Articles about his overland trek appeared in *Time* magazine, *The Washington Post, The Christian Science Monitor* and many others.

In Chicago, Williams and his dogteam made a popular Alaskan exhibit at the Century of Progress Exposition. A *Time* magazine article (October 2, 1933) reported that when former President Herbert Hoover visited the fair he chatted with Williams, and First Lady Eleanor Roosevelt described her meeting with Slim Williams as the most enjoyable part of her visit. A

Leaving the White Roadhouse on Indian River on the way to U.S., 1933
Slim Williams Papers UAF-2007-59-11 University of Alaska Fairbanks

Slim Williams with his leader "Rembrandt." When asked about his name Slim replied, "Well, isn't he a picture?" *Slim Williams Papers UAF-2007-59-16 Univ of AK Fairbanks*

lecture brochure noted: "upon returning to Washington she told newsmen that what she liked best was a tall young man with blue eyes that looked miles away, who had driven his dog team all the way from Alaska."

After the World's Fair closed for the season, Slim and his team of half-bred wolf/dogs proceeded to Washington, D.C., bringing the total distance of his journey by dogteam to over 5,600 miles. He camped in a city park and spent the winter discussing Alaskan concerns with legislators, and even met with President Franklin Roosevelt to further promote the highway. Williams enjoyed a dinner with the President and the First Lady, still advocating for the proposed road. The President finally did set up a commission with Canada to explore building a highway to Alaska, but while the project was considered feasible it was deemed too costly and unnecessary at that time.

Later in life, Slim traveled around the country with his wife doing presentations and slideshows, and he enjoyed success as a popular lecturer, as described in the text of a lecture brochure: "The Adventurers Club of Chicago, where all famous explorers speak, say his talk is one of the most fascinating and thrilling they've had in years."

In 1956 an authorized biography of Slim Williams' adventures was published by Richard Morenus: *Alaska Sourdough: The Story of Slim Williams*. The book detailed Slim's 1933 solo dogsled adventure, and also his 1939 trip from Fairbanks to Seattle by motorcycle with 25-year-old John Logan. Their goal was the New York World's Fair, and just as with Slim's 1933 trip, the purpose was to gain publicity for the need to build a road connecting Alaska to the rest of the United States. At that time, there still wasn't even a crude trail to follow for over 1,000 miles of the journey, so the adventurers crossed the wide rivers and daunting mountains in whatever manner they could, and their much-publicized journey once again spotlighted Alaska's need for a road to the 48 states.

In early 1942, when World War II made an overland route necessary, President Roosevelt signed the authorization, and on November 20, 1942, at Soldier's Summit near Kluane Lake, a ceremony marked completion of the first phase of construction. Today the road is a major artery to the north, and the Alaska Highway project is still heralded as one of the greatest engineering feats of the twentieth century. ~•~

Above: Slim's wheeled sled in the mud between Smithers and Prince George, B.C.
Below: Slim with his team at the Chicago Century of Progress Exposition, 1933
Slim Williams Papers UAF-2007-59-5 (above) and 59-15 (below) University of Alaska Fairbanks

Striking across from the Tanana to the Kantishna, en route to Denali. Hudson Stuck, Harry Karstens, Walter Harper, Robert C. Tatum, Johnny, and Easias departed from Nenana on March 17, 1913. The reached the summit of McKinley on June 7, 1913.

Archdeacon of the Yukon

Ten Thousand Miles with a Dogsled

Hudson Stuck, an Episcopal clergyman and social reformer, was born in London, England in 1865. At the age of 20, eager for wide-open spaces, he tossed a coin: heads for Australia, tails for Texas. It landed tails, and over the course of the next twenty years Stuck earned a name for himself in the Lone Star State. In 1889 he enrolled to study theology, and became an Episcopal priest in 1892.

Once again seeking new adventures, he moved to Alaska in 1904, then nearly 40 years old. Appointed Archdeacon of the Yukon and the Arctic, he traveled incessantly throughout the interior of Alaska, by dogsled in winter and by boat in summer, ministering to those in need.

In 1913 he organized and co-led, with Harry Karstens, the first successful complete ascent of the highest peak in North America, the South Peak of Mount McKinley (Denali), and it is that trek for which he is justifiably famous. But in the preface to his book on the historic climb, *The Ascent of Denali, The 1913 Expedition that First Conquered Mt. McKinley*, Stuck shared his perspective and his true concern: "The author would add, perhaps quite unnecessarily, yet lest any should mistake, a final personal note. He is no professed explorer or climber or 'scientist,' but a missionary, and of these matters an amateur only. The vivid recollection of a back bent down with burdens and lungs at the limit of their function makes him hesitate to describe this enterprise as recreation. It was the most laborious undertaking with which he was ever connected; yet it was done for the pleasure of doing it, and the pleasure far outweighed the pain. But he is concerned much more with men than mountains, and would say, since 'out of the fullness of the heart the mouth speaketh,' that his especial and growing concern, these ten years past, is with the native people of Alaska, a gentle and kindly race, now threatened with a wanton and senseless extermination, and sadly in need of generous champions if that threat is to be averted."

Archdeacon Hudson Stuck and Walter Harper at Allakaket, March, 1917.
Frederick B. Drane Collection UAF-1991-46-531 University of Alaska Fairbanks

Hudson Stuck became a great champion for the native Alaskan Indians and Eskimos, traveling the great rivers, traversing the towering mountains, and guiding his dogteam across vast expanses of frozen tundra from village to village, seeking out the places where his services were most needed. His first trip, during the winter of 1905-06, went from Fairbanks to Circle, Fort Yukon, Bettles, Coldfoot, Kotzebue Sound, Nome and back to Fairbanks over the course of four and a half months. Three years later a shorter trip was made over the Koyukuk River to a new mission at Allakaket for Christmas. In the winter of 1909-10 a journey was made from Fort Yukon to Allakaket, Tanana, Rampart City, Nenana, Chena, Fairbanks, Salchaket, Eagle, Circle, and back to Fort Yukon during a very severe winter.

The winter of 1910-11, the Archdeacon traveled from Tanana to Iditarod and Fort Yukon. Archdeacon Stuck wrote about his travels: "So far as mere distance is concerned... there is nothing noteworthy in this record. There are many men in Alaska who have done much more. A mail-carrier on one of the longer dog routes will cover four thousand miles in a winter, while the writer's average is less than two thousand. But his sled has gone far off the beaten track, across the arctic wilderness, into many remote corners; wherever, indeed, white men or natives were to be found in all the great interior."

Hudson Stuck's accounts of travel methods, especially those pertaining to sled dogs, have become favorite passages among those who still race and travel with dogs. For example, his description of loading dogs is very instructive: "Five dogs are usually considered the minimum team, and seven dogs make a good team. A good, quick-traveling load for a dog team is fifty pounds to the dog, on ordinary trails. The dogs will pull as much as one hundred pounds apiece or more, but that becomes more like freighting than traveling. On a good level trail with strong big dogs, men sometimes haul two hundred pounds to the dog. These, however, are 'gee-pole propositions,' in the slang of the trail, and the man is doing hard work with a band around his chest and the pole in his hand. For quick traveling, fifty pounds to the dog is enough."

Hudson Stuck harbored an appreciation for the sled dogs who transported him across Alaska: "Indeed, any man of feeling who spends the winters with a dog team must grow to a deep sympathy with the animals, and to a keen, sometimes almost a poignant, sense of what he owes to them. There is a mystery about domestic animals of whatever kind. It is a mystery that man should be able to impose his will upon them, change their habits and characters, constrain them to his tasks, take up all their lives with unnatural toil. And that he should get affection and devotion in return makes the mystery yet more mysterious." ~•~

February, 1919. Substituting for Archdeacon Hudson Stuck. Enroute Allakaket. Ala Kellum and team of Archdeacon Stuck. Frederick B. Drane Collection UAF-1991-46-521

Baldy of Nome. Lomen Bros. Photograph P-28-101 Alaska State Library

Baldy of Nome

Scotty Allan's Legendary Leader

In Esther Birdsall Darling's classic book, *Baldy of Nome*, a story is told of a driverless dog team in the 60-mile-long Solomon Derby, a race between Nome and Solomon along the coast of the Bering Sea. The young leader of the team, realizing his driver is missing, turns the team around and returns along the trail, searching...

"Far away in the whiteness, Baldy saw a black spot toward which he sped with mad impatience. It grew more and more distinct, till, beside it, he saw that it was his master, lying pale, motionless and blood-stained in the trail. From a deep gash on his head a crimson stream oozed and froze, matting his hair and the fur on his parka. Baldy stopped short, quivering with an unknown dread. There was something terrifying in the tense body, so still, so mute. He licked the pallid face, the cold hands, and placed a gentle paw upon the man's breast, scratching softly to see if he could not gain some response. There was no answer to his loving appeal; and throwing back his head, there broke from him the weird, wild wail of the Malamute, his inheritance from some wolf ancestor. The other dogs joined the mournful chorus, and then, as it died away, he tried again and again to rouse his silent master. Moment after moment passed, the time seemed endless; but finally the warm tongue and the insistent paw did their work; for there was a slight movement, a flicker of the eyelids, and then Scotty lifted himself upon his elbow and spoke to them."

The incident is based on an actual event, when Scotty, leaning over his sled to look at a broken runner, hit his head on an iron trail marker and was knocked unconscious. Scotty Allan's team, with Baldy in the lead, went on to win the race, and Baldy's rescue made him a hero. The story is even more remarkable because Scotty Allan's regular lead dog, named Kid, had passed away only the evening before the race, and Baldy, who had never led in a race before, had been selected to take his place.

Allan Alexander Allan, who'd been known as Scotty since he was a lad, had set out for the Klondike goldfields and found work moving supplies over the dangerous trails to the mining camps, earning a reputation in the Dawson area as a top notch dog driver. When gold was discovered on the beaches of Nome, Scotty, like many others, traveled down the frozen Yukon River some 1,200 miles to the new goldfields.

Scotty Allan didn't strike it rich in Nome, so he focused on his specialty, training dogs. He took in dogs others didn't want and trained them to race, and he said, "Dogs are the most

Allan and Darling team, Scotty Allan, driver, in the fifth All Alaska Sweepstakes, 1912. Baldy is the near swing dog, behind the leaders.

Scotty Allan and Baldy   A.A. Scotty Allan, ASL-P307-0333

intuitive creatures alive. They take the disposition of their driver. That is why I never let my dogs know that I am tired. At the end of the day…, I sing to the little chaps and whistle so they always reach the end of the trail with their tails up and waving."

In 1907, the dog drivers in Nome banded together to form the Nome Kennel Club to improve the care and breeding of sled dogs. Around this same time Scotty reputedly purchased a sled dog named Baldy from a young boy who could no longer afford to care for him. As Scotty wrote in his autobiography, *Gold, Men and Dogs*, he was one of the founders of the All-Alaska Sweepstakes, the first organized sled dog race, which ran from Nome to Candle, a distance of 408 miles, from the shore of the Bering Sea to the shore of the Arctic Ocean

The first All Alaska Sweepstakes race took five days to finish and was won by John Hegness. The next year Scotty Allan and Baldy took first place, repeating the win again in 1911 and 1912, and they placed in the top three a total of eight times. In five other races, they finished either second or third, and they became famous beyond Alaska, all across the United States. Their race entries were followed and reported in national newspapers such as *The New York Times*.

As Allan and Baldy gained fame, Allan partnered with his sponsor, Esther Birdsall Darling, to form the Allan and Darling Kennel, which became one of the best-known racing kennels in Alaska. Allan's dogs were so well known that when the United States entered World War I, the government commissioned dogs from the Allan and Darling Kennel to haul supplies for the French military. Twenty-eight of Baldy's sons and grandsons were chosen, bringing the total dogs from Nome to over 100. When they were ready to leave Nome, the whole group of dogs were put on a single 350 ft. gangline, and Scotty Allan's lead dog Spot led the 106-dog team through the streets of town to board the waiting ship.

Scotty Allan would go on to be elected to the Alaska Territorial Legislature in 1917 and 1919, and Admiral Richard Byrd sought out Scotty to train the dogs for Byrd's 1928 Antarctica Expedition. Scotty and his family moved to California prior to the 1925 Diphtheria Epidemic in Nome, which resulted in the famous Serum Run. They took the venerable old leader Baldy with them, and the famous sled dog lived out the remainder of his days in the warm California sunshine.

On April, 15th, 1922 *The New York Times* reported Baldy's death to their readers: "Berkeley, Cal., April 14.-- Baldy of Nome, famed for the races he won in Alaska, his heroic deeds that have been twenty-eight Malamute sons and grand-put in prose and verse, and for the sons he gave to France for the World War, was buried here today. He died in a dog hospital of old age and his final resting place is under the rose-bushes in the garden of 'Scotty' Allan, whose life he once saved. Baldy was 15 years old. He was two years old when Allan 'mushed' him through the first of his seven races for the All-Alaska Sweepstakes of 418 miles. With Baldy as the leader, Allan was brought in winner six times." ~•~

Baldy of Nome. Photo: Walter B. Pond, Juneau, Alaska. P87-2606 Alaska State Library

A Dog-Puncher on the Yukon

Arthur Treadwell Walden

"Let me tell you about this man Walden. He reached the country of the Yukon in the early part of '96, when Circle City was the center and the Birch Creek mines the magnet. Always an understanding companion of dogs, he was soon hauling freight across the white wilderness with dog-team.

"This was the Alaska before the days of the Klondike, the frontier of the miners' meetings and the sourdough, the land of justice and order without laws or statutes, the period of the gambling hall that was strict and square. Walden saw and took part in it all." -author and anthropologist Walter Collins O'Kane, from the Introduction to *A Dog-Puncher on the Yukon*

Arthur Treadwell Walden was a pioneering dog driver, a Klondike Gold Rush adventurer, developer of the Chinook sled dog breed, founder of the New England Sled Dog Club, and a major participant in the first Byrd Antarctic Expedition. He wrote a book about his adventures in Alaska and the Klondike, titled *A Dog-Puncher on the Yukon*, along with the instructive *Harness and Pack,* and *Leading a Dog's Life*.

Born in Indianapolis, Indiana, on May 10, 1871, he was the son of the Rev. Treadwell Walden, an Episcopal clergyman, and Elizabeth Leighton Walden. He was educated at Chattuck Military School in Faribault, Minnesota, and in 1890 he went to Boston, Massachusetts, where he visited the kin of his father's second wife, a well-to-do newspaper family named Sleeper. Through this connection Arthur Walden met Katherine Sleeper, and was hired as manager of her 1,300-acre Wonalancet Farm in New Hampshire.

In 1896, at the age of 24 and driven by a keen sense of adventure, Walden left Wonalancet and headed to the gold fields of Alaska. He worked at several jobs, including prospector, logger, stevedore, river pilot, and finally, hauling freight by dogsled, known in the Circle City area as 'dog-punching.' In *A Dog-Puncher on the Yukon*, Walden described the sleds and loads which were typical of the day: "The ordinary freight outfit consisted of three full-sized sleds, one behind the other, drawn up close and connected by cross-chains, making each sled follow in exactly the same track as the sled ahead of it. The sleds had to be so strongly made and heavily braced with iron that each weighed from sixty to eighty pounds, the front one being the heaviest. They were loaded for an average team with six hundred, four hundred, and two hundred pounds apiece, thus making a total of twelve hundred pounds, or about two hundred pounds per dog."

Arthur Walden saw the new century in carrying freight,

Arthur Walden and Chinook

supplies and mail on the Yukon River, and he was the first to bring news of the Klondike gold strike to Circle City, Alaska. He spent seven years freighting with dog teams, returning to Wonalancet and marrying Kate Sleeper in December of 1902. Having seen what sled dogs were capable of, Walden wanted to continue mushing, but in New England, horses and oxen were the draft animals of choice; quality sled dogs were not available. So Walden began a breeding program at Wonalancet, striving for dogs that possessed his ideal combination of strength, speed, endurance, and good nature.

While in the Yukon Walden had worked with a dog named Chinook, whose qualities he admired and wanted to develop in his line of sled dogs. In January 1917 his efforts produced a trio of pups he named Rikki, Tikki and Tavi, after the brave mongoose in Rudyard Kipling's classic, *Jungle Book*. As he grew, Rikki exhibited the traits that Walden had been seeking, and he renamed the dog Chinook, honoring the dog that had so impressed him in the Yukon. A descendent of Admiral Peary's famous husky, Polaris, Chinook became the foundation stud of Chinook Kennels, and Walden's constant companion.

Walden was a born promoter, and soon his Chinook sled dogs were gaining renown far and wide. In 1922 he persuaded a local paper company to sponsor the first Eastern International Dog Derby of 123 miles, bringing the sport of dogsled racing to New England. Two years later he spearheaded the founding of the New England Sled Dog Club, serving as its first president. In 1927 at Poland Spring, Maine, Walden's team went up against Leonhard Seppala, hero of the Nome Serum Run, but he lost the race to Seppala's team despite a series of misadventures experienced on the trail by the All Alaska Sweepstakes champion and his dogs.

Around that same time, Walden heard of Rear Admiral Richard E. Byrd's plans for a major Antarctic expedition, and after meeting with Byrd, Walden was appointed the lead trainer and driver of dog teams for the expedition. During the winter of late 1927 and early 1928, the dogs and drivers gathered at Walden's Wonalancet Farm to begin training. Winter survival gear was tested in the harsh conditions of New Hampshire's White Mountains, and in September, 1928 the teams went to Antarctica.

The expedition landed on Christmas Day and for the next three months Walden and nine other drivers freighted 650 tons of gear from the ships to the base camp at Little America. Byrd wrote in his book, *Little America*: "Had it not been for the dogs, our attempts to conquer the Antarctic must have ended in failure. On January 17th, Walden's single team of thirteen dogs moved 3,500 pounds of supplies from ship to base, a distance of 16 miles each trip, in two journeys. Walden's team was the backbone of our transport. Seeing him rush his heavy loads along the trail, outstripping the younger men, it was difficult to believe that he was an old man. He was 58 years old, but he had the determination and strength of youth."

Unfortunately, midway through the expedition, on his 12th birthday, January 17, 1929, Chinook inexplicably disappeared. Walden had wanted to bury his great friend in his harness, but Chinook's body was never found. Upon returning to Wonalancet in 1930, he learned a highway was being developed on the old trail which Chinook had travelled with his team countless times over the years. Walden requested the road be named the Chinook Trail, the name it bears to this day.

Clearly ahead of his time in anticipating the sport of mushing, Walden wrote in 1927: "People in general have an idea that dog driving is confined to racing, since sport of any kind is first to break into print, but this is not so. The greatest pleasure is the driving. The whole of northern New England lies open to the man who has a team of from two dogs up, at a time when some of its most attractive parts are practically closed for the winter months for all modes of travel except by dog team. The whole mountain section of northern Vermont, and the lake region of Maine are some of the most attractive sections for this health-giving sport of anywhere in America." ~•~

A team of Walden's Chinook sled dogs, around 1920.

Bibliography

The web sites listed in this bibliography give access to the books and documents which are available to read free online (please type URLs carefully). For the web sites of authors and the publishers of the other listed books, please see the Resources section on page 82.

Allen, Allan Alexander. *Gold, Men and Dogs.* G. P. Putnam's sons, 1931.

Bell, Karen, and Janet Shelfer. *Taku: Four Amazing Individuals, Four Incredible Life Stories, and the Alaskan Wilderness Lodge That Brought Them Together.* Will Publishing, 2006.

Brown, Tricia. *Iditarod Country: Exploring the Route of the Last Great Race.* Epicenter Press, 1998.

Bucki, Carrie. *Reindeer Roundup: Reindeer History in Alaska.* Reindeer Research Program, University of Alaska Fairbanks, 2004
http://reindeer.salrm.uaf.edu/about_reindeer/history.php

Byrd, Richard Evelyn. *Little America: Aerial Exploration in the Antarctic, The Flight to the South Pole.* G.P. Putnam's Sons, 1930.

Caldwell, Elsie. *Alaska Trail Dogs.* Smith. 1945.

Cole, Terrence. *Nome: City of Golden Beaches.* Alaska Geographic Society, 1984.

Coppinger, Lorna. *The World of Sled Dogs: From Siberia to Sport Racing.* Howell Book House, 1977.

Crosby, Alfred W. *America's Forgotten Pandemic: The Influenza of 1918.* Cambridge University Press, 2003.

Dawson Daily News, July 8, 1912.
http://ycdl4.yukoncollege.yk.ca/~agraham//news/wada.htm

Darling, Esther Birdsall. *The Great Dog Races of Nome Official Souvenir History 1916.* Nome Kennel Club, 1916. http://yukondigitallibrary.ca/digitalbook/greatdogracesnome/

Darling, Esther Birdsall. *Baldy of Nome.* A.M. Robertson, 1913.
http://www.gutenberg.org/files/11758/11758-h/11758-h.htm

Darling, Esther Birdsall. *Boris: Grandson of Baldy.* Alfred A. Knopf, 1946.

Darling, Esther Birdsall. *Navarre of the North: A Thrilling Story of the Grandson of Baldy of Nome.* The Sun Dial Press, 1930.

Dean, Charles L. *Soldiers and Sled Dogs: A History of Military Dog Mushing.* University of Nebraska Press, 2005.

Farley, Howard. *History of the Nome Kennel Club.*
http://www.nomekennelclub.com/nkchistory.htm

Freedman, Lew. *Iditarod Classics: Tales of the Trail Told by the Men and Women Who Race Across Alaska.* Epicenter Press, 1992.

Freedman, Lew. *Yukon Quest: The Story of the World's Toughest Sled Dog Race.* Epicenter Press, 2010.

Garst, Shannon. *Scotty Allan, King of the Dog-Team Drivers.* Julian Messner, 1946.

Greiner, Mary Anne. *Mary Joyce: Taku to Fairbanks, 1,000 Miles by Dogteam.* Authorhouse, 2007.

Hegener, Helen. *The Yukon Quest Album.* Northern Light Media, 2010.

Hegener, Helen. *The Stained Glass Dog Team.* Northern Light Media, 2012.

Hegener, Mark and Helen. *All Alaska Sweepstakes.* Northern Light Media, 2009.

Henderson, Joe. *Retracing Leffingwell, Part I. Mushing Magazine,* July/August, 2006.
http://www.alaskanarcticexpedition.com/articles/Retracing_Leffingwell.pdf

Henderson, Joe. *Retracing Leffingwell, Part II. Mushing Magazine,* Sept/Oct, 2007.
http://www.alaskanarcticexpedition.com/articles/Retracing_Leffingwell_Part_2.pdf

Henderson, Joe. *Retracing Leffingwell, Part III. Mushing Magazine,* Nov/Dec, 2008
http://www.alaskanarcticexpedition.com/articles/Retracing_Leffingwell_Part_3.pdf

Leffingwell, Ernest de Koven. *A Communication from Leffingwell.*
https://play.google.com/store/books/details?id=OLMiAQAAIAAJ

Lemish, Michael G. *War Dogs: A History of Loyalty and Heroism.* Potomac Books, 1999.

London, Jack. *The Call of the Wild.* Macmillan, 1903.
http://en.wikisource.org/wiki/The_Call_of_the_Wild_(London)

Mackey, Lance, et al. *The Lance Mackey Story.* Zorro Books, 2010.

Mangelsdorf, Katie. *Champion of Alaskan Huskies: Joe Redington Sr., Father of the Iditarod.* Publication Consultants, 2011.

Marsh, Kenneth L. *The Trail: The Story of the Historic Valdez-Fairbanks Trail that Opened Alaska's Vast Interior.* Trapper Creek Museum, 2008

Martin, Von. *A Long Way to Nome.* Call of the Wild Huskies Books, 2009.

McLain, Carrie. *Gold Rush Nome.* Portland Graphic Arts Center, 1969.

Mikkelsen, Ejnar; Leffingwell, Ernest de Koven; Howe, George Plummer. *Conquering the Arctic Ice.* W. Heinemann, 1909.

Morenus, Richard. *Alaska Sourdough: The Story Of Slim Williams.* Rand McNally, 1956.

Murphy, Claire Rudolf and Jane G. Haigh. *Gold Rush Dogs.* Alaska Northwest Books, 2001.

National Geographic Magazine. article: *Mankind's Best Friend,* by Ernest Harold Baynes. March, 1919. http://books.google.com/books?id=4RsXAQAAIAAJ

Noice, Harold. *With Stefansson in the Arctic.* Dodd, Mead & Co., New York, 1924.

Olympic Winter Games Committee. *Official Report for the 1932 Winter Olympics.* http://www.la84foundation.org/6oic/OfficialReports/1932/1932w.pdf

Olson, Dean F. *Alaska Reindeer Herdsmen: A Study of Native Management in Transition.* Institute of Social, Economic and Government Research. University of Alaska Fairbanks, 1969 http://www.alaskool.org/projects/reindeer/history/iser1969/RDEER_1.html

Palmer, Frederick. *In the Klondyke: Including an Account of a Winter's Journey to Dawson.* Charles Scribner's Sons. 1899. http://archive.org/details/inklondykeinclu01palmgoog

Perry, Rod. *Trailbreakers: Pioneering Alaska's Iditarod, Vol. 1.* Rod Perry Books, 2009.

Perry, Rod. *Trailbreakers: Pioneering Alaska's Iditarod, Vol. 2.* Rod Perry Books, 2010.

Rennick, Penny, Ed. *Dogs of the North.* Alaska Geographic Society, 1987.

Ricker, Elizabeth Miller. *Seppala: Alaskan Dog Driver.* Little, Brown, and Company. 1930.

Salisbury, Gay and Salisbury, Laney. *The Cruelest Miles: The Heroic Story of Dogs and Men in a Race Against an Epidemic.* W. W. Norton & Company, 2003.

Shields, Mary. *Sled Dog Trails.* Pyrola Publishers, 1984.

Schneider, William. *On Time Delivery: The Dog Team Mail Carriers.* University of Alaska Press, 2012.

Stuck, Hudson. *Ten Thousand Miles with a Dogsled: A Narrative of Winter Travel in Interior Alaska.* Charles Scribner's Sons, 1914.
http://www.gutenberg.org/ebooks/22965

Stuck, Hudson. *The Ascent of Denali (Mt. McKinley): A Narrative of the First Complete Ascent of the Highest Peak in North America.* Charles Scribner's Sons, 1914.
http://www.gutenberg.org/ebooks/26059

Swan, Thomas. *Marche: Sledge Dogs in the Northwest Fur Trade.*
http://www.tworiversak.com/sleddoghx1.htm

Tani, Yuji. *The Samurai Dog-Musher Under the Northern Lights.* Japan: Yama to Keikoku, 1995.

Vaudrin, Bill. *Racing Alaskan Sled Dogs.* Alaska Northwest Publishing Co., 1976.

Walden, Arthur Treadwell. *A Dog-Puncher on the Yukon.* Houghton Mifflin Co., 1928.

White, Tim. *A History of Mushing Before We Knew It.*
http://sleddogsport.net/index.php?option=com_content&task=view&id=16&Itemid=29

Wickersham, James. *Old Yukon: Tales, Trails, and Trials.* Washington Law Book Company, 1938.

Willoughby, Barrett. *Alaskans All.* Houghton Mifflin, 1933.

Wirt, Loyal. *Alaskan Adventures: A Tale of Our Last Frontier, and of 'Whiskers', Gallant Leader of the First Dog Team to Cross Alaska.* Revell. 1937.

Resources

Websites

- **B.A.R.K.**

  Buy A Round of Kibble

  http://www.sleddogcentral.com/bark.htm

- **Go Mush**

  "Stay on Track"

  http://gomush.com

- **Iditarod Trail Sled Dog Race**

  "The Last Great Race"

  http://iditarod.com

- **Northern Light Media**

  Races, Articles, History, Book Reviews

  http://northernlightmedia.com

- **Mushing Magazine**

  "Magazine of Dog-Powered Adventure"

  http://www.mushing.com/

- **Sled Dog Central**

  "Advertising and information since 1997"

  http://sleddogcentral.com/

- **Team & Trail**

  Mushing news

  http://www.alaskadispatch.com/section/team-and-trail

- **Yukon Quest**

  "The World's Toughest Sled Dog Race"

  http://yukonquest.com

Photographs

    The photographs in this book are from several sources, primarily the Alaska State Library archive collections, which are accessible online via the Alaska State Library Historical Collections: "A presence in Alaska since 1891, Alaska State Library's Historical Collections is mandated by statute to collect and preserve Alaska's history. The Collections' Territorial, State, Russian American, Native language and primary source materials form a major reference and research repository, an information center for state government and a comprehensive visual portrait of the State. The University of Alaska Fairbanks' Alaska and Polar Regions Collections contain one of the world's largest collections of historic photographs, manuscripts, moving images, rare books, maps, oral histories, and printed materials pertaining to Alaska and the Polar regions. Spanning six centuries, the materials document a wide variety of topics including politics, religion, the Alaska Gold Rush, settlement, Alaska Native history and culture, and Arctic social, natural, and physical sciences."

    The Alaska Virtual Library and Digital Archives are accessible at the web address http://vilda.alaska.edu — their collections represent thousands of primary Alaskan source materials covering a broad range of topics.

    Other photo sources included the Creative Commons, a nonprofit organization that enables the sharing and use of creativity and knowledge through free legal tools, and the Wikimedia Commons, which is a media file repository making available public domain and freely-licensed educational media content. It acts as a common repository for the various projects of the Wikimedia Foundation. The repository is created and maintained by volunteers. The scope of Commons is set out on the project scope pages. Unlike traditional media repositories, Wikimedia Commons is free. Everyone is allowed to copy, use and modify any files freely as long as they follow the terms specified by the author; this often means crediting the source and author(s) appropriately and releasing copies/improvements under the same freedom to others. The license conditions of each individual media file can be found on their description page. The Wikimedia Commons database itself and the texts in it are licensed under the Creative Commons Attribution/Share-Alike License.

    Several photographs and images were shared from private collections, including those of Northern Light Media. Many photos were available from multiple sources, and for many others the source has been lost to history. The author welcomes inquiries and information about the photographs in this book, and is actively seeking photos which might be used in future editions.

Timeline

1896 - Arthur Treadwell Walden arrives in Circle City, Alaska
1898 - Klondike Gold Rush, Dawson City, Yukon Territory
1899 - Nome gold rush
　　　　 Reindeer used to deliver mail for the U.S. Postal Service in Alaska
　　　　 Published: *In the Klondyke: A Winter's Journey to Dawson*, by F. Palmer
1901 - Lt. Billy Mitchell uses sled dogs to build a cable/telegraph from WA to AK
1902 - Jujiro Wada arrives in Dawson City with news of Fairbanks gold rush
1903 - Published: *The Call of the Wild*, by Jack London
1904 - Hudson Stuck appointed Archdeacon of the Yukon and the Arctic
1906 - Ernest de Koven Leffingwell begins his Arctic coastal explorations
1907 - Nome Kennel Club founded
1908 - All Alaska Sweepstakes first champion John Hegness
1909 - All Alaska Sweepstakes champion Scotty Allan
　　　　 Jujiro Wada leads a party from Seward to establish the Iditarod Trail
1910 - All Alaska Sweepstakes champion John Johnson
1911 - All Alaska Sweepstakes champion Scotty Allan
1912 - All Alaska Sweepstakes champion Scotty Allan
1913 - All Alaska Sweepstakes champion Fay Dalzene
　　　　 Published: *Baldy of Nome*, by Esther Birdsall Darling
　　　　 Hudson Stuck, Harry Karstens, et al summit Denali's South Peak
1914 - All Alaska Sweepstakes champion John Johnson
　　　　 Leonhard Seppala enters his first All Alaska Sweepstakes race
　　　　 Published: *Ten Thousand Miles with a Dog Sled,* by Hudson Stuck
　　　　 Military sled dogs haul supplies between France and Germany, WWI
1915 - All Alaska Sweepstakes champion Leonhard Seppala
1916 - All Alaska Sweepstakes champion Leonhard Seppala
　　　　 Published: *The Great Dog Races of Nome*, by Esther Birdsall Darling
1917 - All Alaska Sweepstakes champion Leonhard Seppala
1921 - Harry Karstens creates the Mt. McKinley Park Kennel
1925 - Serum Run relayed diphtheria antitoxin from Nenana to Nome

1926 - A statue of Balto is erected in New York City's Central Park
1930 - Siberian Husky breed officially recognized by the AKC
      Published: *Seppala: Alaskan Dog Driver*, by Elizabeth Ricker
1931 - Published: *Gold, Men, and Dogs*, by Allan Alexander 'Scotty' Allan
1932 - Dog mushing demonstration race at the Winter Olympics, Lake Placid, NY
1933 - Slim Williams mushes his dogteam from Alaska to Chicago
1936 - Mary Joyce mushes her dog team from Juneau to Fairbanks
1944 - Col. Norman Vaughn brought sled dogs into France, WWII
1945 - Published: *Alaska Trail Dogs*, by Elsie Caldwell
1946 - First Fur Rendezvous World Championship Sled Dog Race
      First Open North American Sled Dog Race
      Published: *Scotty Allan, King of the Dog-Team Drivers*, by Shannon Garst
1956 - Published: *The Story of Slim Williams*, by Richard Morenus
1963 - Chester Noongwook is last U.S. Mail driver, Gambell to Savoonga
1969 - Published: *Gold Rush Nome*, by Carrie McLain
1972 - Dog mushing was established as the Alaska state sport
1973 - Iditarod first champion Dick Wilmarth
1974 - Iditarod champion Carl Huntington

      Mary Shields is the first woman to run and to finish the Iditarod

1975 - Iditarod champion Emmitt Peters
1976 - Iditarod champion Jerry Riley

      Published: *Racing Alaskan Sled Dogs*, by Bill Vaudrin

1977 - Iditarod champion Rick Swenson

      Published: *The World of Sled Dogs*, by Lorna Coppinger

1978 - Iditarod champion Dick Mackey
1979 - Iditarod champion Rick Swenson
1980 - Iditarod champion Joe May
1981 - Iditarod champion Rick Swenson
1982 - Iditarod champion Rick Swenson
1983 - Iditarod Champion Rick Mackey

      75th Anniversary All Alaska Sweepstakes champion Rick Swenson

1984 - Iditarod champion Dean Osmar

      The first Yukon Quest Sled Dog Race, champion Sonny Lindner

1985 - Iditarod champion Libby Riddles

      Yukon Quest champion Joe Runyan

1986 - Iditarod champion Susan Butcher

1986 - (continued) Yukon Quest champion Bruce Johnson
USPS issues "Dog sled 1920's" stamp as part of Transportation series
1987 - Iditarod champion Susan Butcher
Yukon Quest champion Bill Cotter
1988 - Iditarod champion Susan Butcher
Yukon Quest champion David Monson
1989 - Iditarod champion Joe Runyan
Yukon Quest champion Jeff King
1990 - Iditarod champion Susan Butcher
Yukon Quest champion Vern Halter
1991 - Iditarod champion Rick Swenson
Yukon Quest champion Charlie Boulding
1992 - Iditarod champion Martin Buser
Yukon Quest champion John Schandelmeier
1993 - Iditarod champion Jeff King
Yukon Quest champion Charlie Boulding
1994 - Iditarod champion Martin Buser
Yukon Quest champion Lavon Barve
1995 - Iditarod champion Doug Swingley
Yukon Quest champion Frank Turner
1996 - Iditarod champion Jeff King
Yukon Quest champion John Schandelmeier
1997 - Iditarod champion Martin Buser
Yukon Quest champion Rick Mackey
1998 - Iditarod champion Jeff King
Yukon Quest champion Bruce Lee
1999 - Iditarod champion Doug Swingley
Yukon Quest champion Ramy Brooks
2000 - Iditarod champion Doug Swingley
Yukon Quest champion Aliy Zirkle
2001 - Iditarod champion Doug Swingley
Yukon Quest champion Tim Osmar
2002 - Iditarod champion Martin Buser

Yukon Quest champion Hans Gatt
2003 - Iditarod champion Robert Sorlie
Yukon Quest champion Hans Gatt
2004 - Iditarod champion Mitch Seavey
Yukon Quest champion Hans Gatt
2005 - Iditarod champion Robert Sorlie
Yukon Quest champion Lance Mackey
2006 - Iditarod champion Jeff King
Yukon Quest champion Lance Mackey
2007 - Iditarod champion Lance Mackey
Yukon Quest champion Lance Mackey
2008 - Iditarod champion Lance Mackey
Yukon Quest champion Lance Mackey
100th Anniversary All Alaska Sweepstakes champion Mitch Seavey
2009 - Iditarod champion Lance Mackey
Yukon Quest champion Sebastian Schnuelle
USPS issues Alaska Statehood stamp with Dee Dee Jonrowe's team
2010 - Iditarod champion Lance Mackey
Yukon Quest champion Hans Gatt
2011 - Iditarod champion John Baker
Yukon Quest champion Dallas Seavey
2012 - Iditarod champion Dallas Seavey
Yukon Quest champion Hugh Neff

Index

A Dog-Puncher on the Yukon, 75
Alaska Club, 24
Alaska Dispatch, 48
Alaska Dog Derby, 35
Alaska dog team post, 12
Alaska Highway, 36, 62-65
Alaska Legislature, 9, 32, 73
Alaska State Library photos, 10, 28, 29, 31-37, 43, 44, 70, 72, 73
Alaska Steamship Line, 35
Alaska Trail Dogs, 9
Alcan Highway, 36
All Alaska Sweepstakes, 20, 33, 42-45, 52, 55, 71, 73
Allan and Darling Kennel, 44, 55, 73
Allan, Scotty, 9, 20, 28, 33, 42-45, 55, 70-73
American Kennel Club, 22
Anchorage, 8
Antilarsook, Mary, 32
Anvik Mission, 28
Anvik, 49
Archdeacon of the Yukon, 66-69
Arctic Club, 24
Atwater, Ben, 13
Baird, John, 15
Baldy of Nome, 33, 44, 70-73
Baldy, 9, 55, 70-73
Balto, 20-23, 33
Barnette, E.T., 14, 18
Bering Sea, 12
Bibliography, 78
Birch Creek mines, 74
Board of Trade, 43
Bowers, Don, 47
Brower, Charlie, 14
Burke, Jill, 48
Butcher, Susan, 13
Byrd, Richard E., 39, 56, 73, 76
Caldwell, Elsie, 9
Call of the Wild, The, 7

Candle, 42-45, 72
Carrie McLain Museum, 22, 42, 45
Champion of Alaskan Huskies, 54
Chinook, 74-77
Circle City, 13, 74
Cruelest Miles, The, 9, 28
Crumrine, Josephine, 35
Dalzene, Fay, 45
Darling, Esther Birdsall, 33, 43, 56, 70
Dawson City, 15, 17
Dawson Daily News, 15
Dean, Charles L., 56
Deering herd, 31
Denali, 66
Diphtheria epidemic, 33, 73
Dog team mail, 10-13
Dog team post, 12
Dog team stamps, 13
Dog-puncher, 74
Dog sled on wheels, 62-65
Eagle, 5, 8
Easias, 66
Emiu, 50
Fairbanks, 14, 17, 34
Flaxman Island, 58
Fort Egbert, 55
Fort Gibbon, 8
Freedman, Lew, 46, 49
Freighting with dog teams, 76
Fritz, 20-23
Gambell, 12
Ghosts, 46-48
Gold, Men and Dogs, 28, 42, 72
Great Dog Races of Nome, The, 43
Greiner, Mary Anne, 36
Grenfell, Dr. Wilfred, 30
Harper, Walter, 66
Healy, Michael A., 31
Hegness, John, 45
Henderson, Joe, 60
Hoover, Herbert, 63
Iditarod Trail Sled Dog Race, 13, 45
Iditarod Trail, 8, 11, 13, 15, 46, 54
Iditarod, 15
Introduction, 8

Ivey, Justin, 26, 27
Jackson, Sheldon, 28-33
Japanese explorer, 14
Johnny, 66
Johnson, "Iron Man," 45
Johnson, G.H., 43
Jonrowe, Dee Dee, 13, 48
Joyce, Mary, 34-37
Juneau, 34-37
Kaasen, Gunnar, 21, 33
Kaltag, 28
Kantishna, 66
Karstens, Harry, 66
Katchatag, Doug, 48
Kid, 71
King, Jeff, 45
Klondike gold rush, 24, 32, 71
Klondike gold strike, 76
Klondike, 74
Klott, Kevin, 48
Kollar, Robart, 57
Kuskokwim, 15
Lake Bennett, 13
Lance Mackey Story, The, 49
Lee, Bruce, 49
Leffingwell, Ernest de Koven, 58-61
Lemish, Michael G., 57
Loads hauled, 11
Lomen, Carl J., 32
Lomen Brothers photographs, 28, 32, 53, 70
London, Jack, 7
Mabel, Joe, 24
Mackey, Lance, 45, 49
Malemute Kid, 53
Mangelsdorf, Katie, 54
Mapping arctic coastline, 58-61
Mikkelsen, Eijnar, 58-61
military sled dogs, 54-57
Mitchell, Lt. Billy, 55
MOHAI, 24-27
Morrison Hotel, 24
Mt. McKinley, 66
Mushing Magazine, 61
Navarre, 44
New England Sled Dog Club, 39, 75

Nome Kennel Club, 33, 42-45
Nome, 20, 22, 42-45, 55
Noongwook, Chester, 12
Noongwook, Nathan, 12
Norwood, H.H., 16
Old Woman Cabin, 48
Olympic demonstration sport, 38-41
Peary, Robert, 76
Pedro, Felix, 15
Prize dog team in the Arctic, 8
Prudhoe Bay, 59
Ramsay, Fox Maule, 45
Redington, Joe Sr., 54
Reindeer Act, 32
Reindeer King, 32
Reindeer Queen, 32
Reindeer, 28-33
Rembrandt, 64
Resources, 82
Richardson Trail, 8
Ricker, Elizabeth, 9, 20, 22
Roosevelt, Eleanor, 63
Roosevelt, Franklin D., 39, 64
Salisbury, Gay and Laney, 9, 28
Samurai Musher, 15
Savoonga, 12
Schultz, Jeff, 13
Seattle Stained Glass, 26, 27
Seattle, 24
Seavey, Mitch, 45
Seeley, Eva 'Short,' 40
Seppala, Alaskan Dog Driver, 22
Seppala, Leonhard, 4, 9, 20-23, 33, 38-41, 42-45
Serum Run, 20, 28, 33, 73
Service, Robert, 46
Seward, 8
Seward and Susitna Mail Team, 12
Seward Peninsula, 53
Seward, 18
Shepherd, Ed, 12
Siberia, 31
Siberian husky, 21, 45
Sinrock Mary, 32
Sled dog mail, 10-13
Sled dogs, 9

sleds, 53
Soldier's Summit, 64
Soldiers and Sled Dogs, 56
Split-the-Wind, 50-53
Spot, 73
St. Godard, Emile, 38-41
St. Lawrence Island, 12
Stained glass dog team, 24-27
Stamps, dogteam, 13
Stefansson, Vilhjalmur, 50-53
Stuck, Hudson, 9, 28-33, 66-69
Swenson, Rick, 45
Taku Lodge, 34-37
Tani, Yuji, 15
Tatum, Robert C., 66
Teller, 32
Ten Thousand Miles with a Dog Sled, 9, 28, 66-69
Territorial legislature, 73
Timeline, 84
Togo, 4, 9, 20-23
Tondreau, Frank, 53
Torigai, Fumi, 15
Trail Eater, The, 33
Trophies, 42
Types of sled dogs, 9
Types of sleds, 11
University of Alaska Fairbanks photos, 11, 38, 62-65, 67, 69
U.S. Army, 54
U.S. Mail reindeer teams, 32
U.S. Mail, 8, 10-13
U.S. Postal Service, 10-13
U.S. Revenue Cutter ships, 31
Unalakleet, 48
Van Zyle, Jon, 46
Vaughn, Col. Norman D., 39, 56
Wada, Jujiro, 14-19
Walden, Arthur Treadwell, 74-77
War Dogs, 57
Weight of loads, 11
Wells, Ward, 12
Wheels on dog sled, 62-65
White, Tim, 41
Williams, Slim, 62-65
Willoughby, Barrett, 33

Wolf, 35
Wonalancet Farm, 75
World War I, 18, 44, 45, 54, 73
World War II, 37, 54
Yukon Mail, 5
Yukon Quest, 18, 49
Yukon River, 11, 15, 46, 71
Yukon Territory, 15, 62 74